ON THE THRESHOLD OF EXACT SCIENCE

THE MIDDLE AGES

A SERIES EDITED BY

EDWARD PETERS

Henry Charles Lea Professor of Medieval History
University of Pennsylvania

Edited and Translated
with an Introduction by
Steven D. Sargent

On the Threshold of Exact Science

SELECTED WRITINGS OF ANNELIESE MAIER

ON LATE MEDIEVAL NATURAL PHILOSOPHY

UNIVERSITY OF PENNSYLVANIA PRESS

PHILADELPHIA

1982

All the essays by Anneliese Maier translated in this volume
are reprinted by permission of Edizioni di Storia e Letteratura, Rome.

Library of Congress Cataloging in Publication Data

Maier, Anneliese, 1905–
  On the threshold of exact science.

  (The Middle ages)
  Bibliography: p.
  Includes index.
  Contents: The nature of motion—Causes, forces,
and resistance—The concept of the function in four-
teenth-century physics [etc.]
    1. Science, Medieval—Addresses, essays, lectures.
2. Philosophy, Medieval—Addresses, essays, lectures.
I. Sargent, Steven D. II. Title III. Series.
Q124.97.M3413   509'.02   81–43524
ISBN 0–8122–7831–3   AACR2

Printed in the United States of America

Contents

Preface

The last twenty-five years have seen a remarkable increase in the quantity and quality of literature available to the English-speaking student of medieval science. General introductions, collections of readings, whole treatises, and advanced studies now cover virtually all the fields and major problems of scholastic scientific thought. It seems to me, however, that the theoretical, that is, philosophical, side of medieval science is still comparatively neglected in works on the history of science in English. Anneliese Maier's writings, on the other hand, more than compensate for this deficiency and therefore should be read, sooner or later, by every serious student of the subject. Unfortunately, this more often happens later than sooner because of the language problem. Maier's German is very readable, but until the student has developed the necessary level of proficiency in the language, Maier's studies will literally be a closed book. This collection of essays in translation is meant, therefore, to make some of Maier's writings available to a larger English-speaking audience and to stimulate interest in the philosophical approach to the history of medieval science represented in her works. If, as a result, students begin to read Maier sooner rather than later, I will have accomplished my purpose.

Every translator is aware of the compromises that must be made in expressing in his or her own language the thoughts of another person. On the whole, I have contented myself with following as closely as possible Maier's train of argument and with reproducing as precisely as possible the content of her ideas. Where necessary, her sentences have been restructured or recast into two or more English sentences. Maier's writing style is clear and unadorned, somewhat intense in tone, and exploits the grammatical possibilities for the subordination of ideas available in German but lacking in English. It is never long-winded or artificially complex; the logic of the ideas is always the primary consideration, and the mode of expression plays a secondary, almost utilitarian role. In the translations I have not tried to imitate her style, but have strived for clarity and accuracy.

Among the people who have aided me in this undertaking, the most deserving of my thanks is Dr. Edward Peters, who suggested the project and was always ready with help and encouragement. I also wish to thank Signorina Maddalena De Luca of Edizioni di Storia e Letteratura for permission to publish these translations and Dr. Agostino Paravicini Bagliani for his friendly advice and information. My sincere thanks are also due to Dr. Elisabeth Gleason for her lively interest in this project.

I am also most grateful to the University of Pennsylvania for providing financial support in the form of a Dean's Fellowship for the 1980–81 academic year and to the Department of History for helping to offset the cost of the permissions.

Rome, 1981   STEVEN D. SARGENT

Bibliographical Notes and Abbreviations

In the translations, Maier's footnotes appear in their original form except for minor changes made to ensure clarity. Aristotle's works are cited by their Latin titles. Commentaries on Aristotle's works and on those of other authors (especially Peter Lombard's *Sententiarum libri quattuor*) are cited by the commentator's name and the abbreviated title of the work commentated. A Roman numeral following a Latin title denotes the book *(liber)* of the work cited. The following abbreviations are used in referring to other sections of Latin treatises:

art.	*articulus*
cap.	*capitulum*
comm.	*commentarium*
dist.	*distinctio*
lect.	*lectio*
lib.	*liber*
qu.	*quaestio*
tract.	*tractatus*

Finally, because Maier's works lack formal bibliographies, I have compiled the following table of printed editions of Latin treatises cited in abbreviated form in the footnotes.

Albertus Magnus, *Physica*

Albertus Magnus. *Physicorum libri VIII.* Vol. 3 of his *Opera Omnia.* Ed. A. Borgnet. Paris: Vivès, 1890.

Albert of Saxony,
De caelo et mundo

Albertus de Saxonia. *Questiones in libros de celo et mundo.* Venice: Bonetus Locatellus for O. Scotus, 1492.

———, *Physica*

Albertus de Saxonia. *Acutissime questiones super libros de physica auscultatione.* Venice: J. Pentius, 1504.

Aureoli, *Sent.*

Aureoli, Petrus. *Commentariorum in primum [-quartum] librum Sententiarum.* Rome: Ex typographia Vaticana, 1596–1605.

Averroes, *Physica*

Averroes. *Aristotelis stagiritae de physico auditu libri octo cum Averrois cordubensis variis in eosdem commentariis.* Vol. 4 of *Aristotelis stagiritae omnia quae extant opera.* Venice: Juntas, 1550.

Avicenna, *Sufficientia*

Avicenna. *Sufficientia.* In *Avicenne perhypatici philosophi ac medicorum facile primi opera in lucem redacta.* Venice: Bonetus Locatellus, 1508.

Bradwardine, *Tractatus proportionum*	Bradwardinus, Thomas. *Tractatus proportionum.* In Politus, Bassanus, *Questio de modalibus Bassani Politi . . . Tractatus proportionum Thome Barduardini* [*Braduardini*]. . . . Venice: Bonetus Locatellus, 1505.
Buridan, *Metaphysica*	(Maier does not specify a particular edition. The work is printed in) Buridanus, Johannes. *In metaphysicen Aristotelis Questiones argutissime.* Paris: for I. Badius, 1518.
———, *Physica*	Buridanus, Johannes. *Subtilissime questiones super octo physicorum libros Aristotelis.* Ed. J. Dullaert. Paris: P. LeDru for D. Roce, 1509.
Burley, *Physica*	(Maier cites two editions:) Burlaeus, Gualterus. *Expositio in octo volumina Aristotelis de Physico auditu.* Venice: J. Herbort, 1482.
	———. *Expositio in Aristotelis Physica.* Venice: Bonetus Locatellus for Octavianus Scotus, 1491.
Copernicus, *De revolutionibus*	(Maier does not specify a particular edition. The first edition was:) Copernicus, Nicolaus. *De revolutionibus orbium coelestium libri VI.* Nuremberg: J. Petreius, 1543.

xi

Duns Scotus, *Opus Oxoniense*	Duns Scotus, Joannes. *Quaestiones in librum primum* [*-quartum*] *Sententiarum* [=*Opus Oxoniense*]. Vols. 8–21 of his *Opera Omnia*. Ed. L. Wadding. Paris: Vivès, 1893–94.
———, *Quodlibeta*	Duns Scotus, Joannes. *Quaestiones Quodlibetales*. Vols. 25–26 of his *Opera Omnia*. Ed. L. Wadding. Paris: Vivès, 1895.
Francis of Meyronnes, *Sent.*	Franciscus de Mayronis. *Scripta in quatuor libros Sententiarum*. Venice: Bonetus Locatellus, 1520.
Hervaeus Natalis, *Sent.*	Hervaeus Natalis. *In quattuor Petri Lombardi Sententiarum volumina scripta subtilissima*. Venice: Lazarus de Soardis, 1505.
Johannes Canonicus, *Physica*	Johannes Canonicus. *Quaestiones super Physica Aristotelis*. Venice: Bonetus Locatellus for Octavianus Scotus, 1492/93.
Liber sex principiorum	(Formerly attributed to Gilbert de la Porrée. Maier does not specify a particular edition. A critical edition is now available in:) *Aristoteles Latinus*. Vol. I, 6–7: *Categoriarum Supplementa, Phorphyrii Isagoge et Anonymi Fragmentum vulgo vocatum "Liber Sex Principiorum."* Ed. L. Minio-Paluello. Bruges/Paris: Desclée de Brouwen, 1966.

Ockham, *Philosophia Naturalis*	Ockham, Guillelmus. *Philosophia Naturalis*. Rome: Typis I. B. Robletti, 1637.
———, *Sent.*	Ockham, Guillelmus. *Super quatuor libros sententiarum subtilissime questiones earumdemque decisiones.* Lyon: J. Trechsel, 1495.
Olivi, *Sent.*	Olivi, Petrus Johannis. *Quaestiones in secundum librum sententiarum.* Ed. Bernard Jansen. 3 vols. Quaracchi: Ex typographia Collegii S. Bonaventurae, 1922–26.
Richard of Mediavilla, *Sent.*	Ricardus de Mediavilla. *Super quatuor libros Sententiarum Petri Lombardi quaestiones subtilissimae.* Brescia: Vincentinus Sabbius, 1591.
Siger of Brabant, *Impossibilia*	(Maier does not specify a particular edition. The work is printed in:) *Die Impossibilia des Siger von Brabant.* Ed. Clemens Baeumker. Münster: Aschendorff, 1898.
Suisset [Swineshead], *Calculationes*	Suisset, Ricardus. *Calculationes noviter emendate atque revise.* Venice: O. Scotus's heirs, 1520.

Thomas Aquinas, *Physica*	Thomas de Aquino. *Commentaria in octo libros physicorum Aristotelis.* Vol. 2 of his *Opera Omnia.* Leonine ed. Rome: Ex typographia polyglotta S. C. de propaganda fide, 1884.
Vernias, *Quaestio de gravibus et levibus*	Vernias, Nicoletus. *Quaestio de gravibus et levibus.* In Albertus de Saxonia, *Acutissime questiones super libros de physica auscultatione . . . Nicoleti Verniatis . . . de gravibus et levibus questio subtilissima.* Venice: J. Pentius, 1504.

ON THE THRESHOLD OF EXACT SCIENCE

Introduction

Anneliese Maier was born on November 17, 1905, in Tübingen, where her father, Heinrich Maier, was a professor of philosophy at the university. She attended secondary school in Göttingen and Heidelberg, was graduated in 1923, and then studied philosophy, physics, and history at the universities of Zürich and Berlin. In her dissertation, written under Professor Eduard Spranger at Berlin, she examined Kant's categories of quality from both a historical and a philosophical standpoint. Completed in 1930, it was published in the same year as a supplement to *Kant-Studien*. [1]

Maier's basic intellectual orientation and the concerns of her early career were profoundly influenced by her father's philosophical writings. Heinrich Maier's main work, *Philosophie der Wirklichkeit*, the first volume of which appeared in 1926, presents a systematic metaphysical description of reality, that is, an analysis of the

1. *Kants Qualitätskategorien* (Kant-Studien, Ergänzungsheft 65) (Berlin: Pan-Verlag, K. Metzner, 1930); reprinted in Anneliese Maier, *Zwei Untersuchungen zur nachscholastischen Philosophie* (Rome: Edizioni di Storia e Letteratura, 1968), pp. 71–150.

3

elementary categories and formal structure of reality.[2] Metaphysics was not, however, his only concern; he also wrote works on logic, epistemology, psychology, and history. Anneliese Maier was thoroughly imbued with her father's philosophical and historical approach. In her dissertation she developed in detail an interpretation of Kant's concept of reality only suggested by her father in *Philosophie der Wirklichkeit*. After his death in 1933, she edited and saw through publication the manuscript of the second and third volumes of *Philosophie der Wirklichkeit*, which appeared in 1933 and 1935. In 1937 she wrote a brief intellectual biography of her father for the *Philosophen-Lexikon*, in which she emphasized not only his contributions to metaphysics but also his speculations on the nature of historical knowledge.[3]

A new phase of her career began in 1936, when the Prussian Academy of Sciences, which was in the process of publishing Leibniz's complete works, gave her the task of searching out his extant letters in Italian libraries. In carrying out this assignment she made her first contact with the manuscript and archival collections of the Vatican, from which she later mined the raw material of her major studies. A year after submitting her report on Leibniz,[4] she published her first study of the history of natural philosophy, *Die Mechanisierung des Weltbildes im 17. Jahrhundert.*[5] In it Maier takes issue with the interpretation of the scientific revolution as a linear historical process initiated by the revival of atomism and Galileo's innovations in mechanics, which, accompanied by the increased use of experimentation, gradually produced a new body of scientific thought dependent only on its own laws and assumptions. The outcome of the process is supposed to have been the replacement of

2. Heinrich Maier, *Philosophie der Wirklichkeit*, 3 vols. (Tübingen: Mohr, 1926–35).

3. "Heinrich Maier" in *Philosophen-Lexikon*, ed. W. Ziegenfuss (Berlin: E. S. Mittler, 1937).

4. "Leibnizbriefe in italienischen Bibliotheken," in *Quellen und Forschungen aus italienischen Archiven und Bibliotheken* 27 (1937): 267–82.

5. (Forschungen zur Geschichte der Philosophie und der Pädagogik, Heft 18) (Leipzig: F. Meiner, 1938); reprinted in *Zwei Untersuchungen zur nachscholastischen Philosophie* (Rome: Edizioni di Storia e Letteratura, 1968), pp. 13–67.

a world view derived from speculative philosophy by one based on the exact mathematical description of nature. Maier argues that the process was by no means uniform, but rather the result of numerous interacting lines of development, and that it was in fact more speculative than problem oriented. In her opinion, a philosophical reorientation had to precede the development of a new world view based on mechanical and mathematical principles:

> In fact, it happened the other way around; speculative considerations and philosophical theories were of primary importance. They gave the stimulus in most cases for the use of experiments and for the mathematical description of phenomena, whose results were then used to confirm and enrich or to modify the philosophical positions. . . . If we inquire into the origins, character, and significance of the mechanization of the world picture in the seventeenth century, we must focus our attention on the philosophical systems within which and out of which it developed.[6]

Maier's study examines only one aspect of this large problem—the development of mechanistic explanations of the sense qualities. She begins with a short sketch of the "traditional" theory that was dominant in 1600 and then analyzes the new ideas proposed by a variety of seventeenth-century thinkers, including Gassendi, Galileo, Hobbes, Descartes, Huygens, Newton, Leibniz, Boyle, and Locke. The introductory section on the "traditional" doctrine represents Maier's first published encounter with scholastic-Aristotelian natural philosophy. In it she assesses the state of the theory of qualities ca. 1600 in order to show that the mechanistic approach was as yet unconsidered. For the content of the premechanistic theory she relies mainly on the scholastics Suárez (1548–1617) and Zabarella (1533–1589) and on two secondary works: Pierre Duhem's *Études sur Léonard de Vinci*, 3 vols. (Paris: Hermann, 1906–13) and Konstanty Michalski's "La physique nouvelle et les différents courants philosophiques au XIVe siècle," *Bulletin de l'académie polonaise des sciences et des lettres*, Classe d'histoire et de philosophie, année 1927 (Cracow: Imprimerie de l'Université, 1928). The study as a whole

6. Ibid., p. 4 (1968 ed.: pp. 15–16).

deals with the various positions taken in the rejection of the scholastic theory of sense qualities and can be viewed in part as a supplement to her dissertation. But it also represents an important stage in her intellectual development, since it contains in her summary of the "traditional" approach and in her citation of Duhem and Michalski the earliest indications of her interest in the field that would ultimately become the focus of her research. Moreover, we see already in this study an emphasis on the philosophical aspects of the history of science that are so prominent in her later work.

After 1937 Maier settled in Rome and began the close association with the Vatican Library that characterized the rest of her career. There she became acquainted with Msgr. Auguste Pelzer, who took an active interest in her studies and gave her the benefit of his extensive knowledge of the library's holdings. Both he and Cardinal Giovanni Mercati pointed out to her the existence of numerous unexploited manuscript treatises on natural philosophy in the Vatican collections, and their help and support played a major role in her decision to pursue her philosophical and scientific interests back into the thirteenth and fourteenth centuries. In 1939 she published her first monograph on scholastic natural philosophy, *Das Problem der intensiven Grösse in der Scholastik* (Leipzig: Keller, 1939), and thereafter hardly a year went by in which she did not make some contribution to the field. Between 1939 and 1949 she examined in a series of essays and studies many of the most fundamental problems and concepts of late medieval scientific thought: the problem of intensive magnitude, the theory of impetus, the structure of matter, gravitation, the latitude of forms, the theory of motion, the theory of the continuum, the quantity of matter, functions and the laws of motion, the problem of infinity, and Nicole Oresme's geometry of qualities and motions. She considered them, moreover, from the standpoint of both philosophical content and historical development. Later, as she discovered new manuscript sources and became acquainted with an ever-wider range of treatises and commentaries, Maier returned to some of these same questions and treated them in more detail, although in almost every case the basic conclusions of these pioneering studies remained unchanged.

During the war Maier stayed in Rome, and when her funds from

Germany were cut off, Cardinal Mercati supported her out of his own resources. In 1950 she was appointed to a professorship at the University of Cologne, but after teaching there one year she decided to return to Rome. In 1954 she was made a fellow of the Max-Planck-Institut and thereafter was able to pursue her research without interruption.

Because they appeared during the war or in a variety of different journals, Maier's early monographs and essays were difficult to obtain and did not reach a wide audience.[7] It was thus an event of major importance when the publisher of Edizioni di Storia e Letteratura, Don Giuseppe De Luca, undertook both to reprint many of her existing studies and to publish the results of her ongoing research. A total of nine volumes ultimately appeared as part of the series "Storia e Letteratura": five volumes of her "Studien zur Naturphilosophie der Spätscholastik" (studies on late scholastic natural philosophy); three of *Ausgehendes Mittelalter,* her collected essays on fourteenth-century intellectual history; and one containing "Die Mechanisierung des Weltbildes" and "Kants Qualitätskategorien."[8] As a result of this initiative, Maier's works were made available to

7. In *Isis* 40 (1949): 120–21, E. J. Dijksterhuis notes that her books "have remained comparatively unknown."

8. All these works are still in print and available from Edizioni di Storia e Letteratura, Via Lancellotti 18, 00186 Roma.

"Studien zur Naturphilosophie der Spätscholastik"

1. *Die Vorläufer Galileis im 14. Jahrhundert,* 2d ed. rev. (Storia e Letteratura, 22) (Rome: Edizioni di Storia e Letteratura, 1966).

2. *Zwei Grundprobleme der scholastischen Naturphilosophie: das Problem der intensiven Grösse, die Impetustheorie,* 3rd ed., rev. and exp. (Storia e Letteratura, 37) (Rome: Edizioni di Storia e Letteratura, 1968).

3. *An der Grenze von Scholastik und Naturwissenschaft: die Struktur der materiellen Substanz, das Problem der Gravitation, die Mathematik der Formlatituden,* 2d ed. (Storia e Letteratura, 41) (Rome: Edizioni di Storia e Letteratura, 1952).

4. *Metaphysische Hintergründe der spätscholastischen Naturphilosophie* (Storia e Letteratura, 52) (Rome: Edizioni di Storia e Letteratura, 1955).

5. *Zwischen Philosophie und Mechanik* (Storia e Letteratura, 69) (Rome: Edizioni di Storia e Letteratura, 1958).

Ausgehendes Mittelalter. Gesammelte Aufsätze zur Geistesgeschichte des 14. Jahrhun-

other scholars interested in medieval intellectual history, and her reputation as a meticulous and thorough researcher was firmly established.

The "Studien zur Naturphilosophie der Spätscholastik" comprise the main body of Maier's researches into scholastic science and natural philosophy. The first volume, *Die Vorläufer Galileis im 14. Jahrhundert,* published in 1949, is in format the most comprehensive of the five works. In it Maier examines fourteenth-century scientific thought under three main headings: basic principles and concepts, problems of mathematical and physical theory, and changes in world view. Her purpose is to describe the achievements of medieval scientific thought without making anachronistic judgments about its modernity and to understand in what sense the natural philosophers of the fourteenth century were "Galileo's predecessors." In many respects *Die Vorläufer Galileis* defines the approach and sets the tone for all the later studies. Two of the ten chapters (nos. 1 and 4) are revised versions of essays published earlier, and chapter 7 incorporates parts of two other essays, but for the most part the studies in the volume appeared there for the first time.

In 1951 the revised versions of two earlier monographs concerning the problem of intensive magnitude and the theory of impetus were published together as the second volume of the *Studien* with the title *Zwei Grundprobleme der scholastischen Naturphilosophie.* Of the five volumes of the *Studien,* this one is still perhaps the most famous

---

derts, 3 vols. (Storia e Letteratura, 97, 105, 138) (Rome: Edizioni di Storia e Letteratura, 1964, 1967, 1977).

Zwei Untersuchungen zur nachscholastischen Philosophie: Die Mechanisierung des Weltbildes im 17. Jahrhundert, Kants Qualitätskategorien (Storia e Letteratura, 112) (Rome: Edizioni di Storia e Letteratura, 1968).

A bibliography of Anneliese Maier's publications compiled by A. Paravicini Bagliani can be found in *Ausgehendes Mittelalter* 3:615–26.

The continuing influence of Maier's research is demonstrated by the contributions to the memorial volume recently published in her honor: *Studi sul XIV Secolo in Memoria di Anneliese Maier,* ed. A. Maierù and A. Paravicini Bagliani (Storia e Letteratura, 151) (Rome: Edizioni di Storia e Letteratura, 1981). This book also includes an updated bibliography of Maier's writings.

because Maier's study of the theory of impetus is a model of careful and thorough scholarship on a subject that had previously been treated in a superficial or one-sided manner. The third volume, *An der Grenze von Scholastik und Naturwissenschaft* (1952), is the second edition of three studies first published in 1943 which examine the scholastic theories of the structure of matter, gravitation, and the latitude of forms.

In *Metaphysische Hintergründe der spätscholastischen Naturphilosophie* (1955), the fourth volume of the *Studien*, Maier turns her attention to the underlying metaphysical structures of late scholastic philosophy. Although the chapters are based in part on earlier investigations, particularly in her discussions of the concept of time and the theory of inexhaustible forces, in general the volume represents a step beyond her previous work. Instead of considering specific physical theories, Maier analyzes the metaphysical assumptions that characterize the fourteenth-century approach to natural phenomena and that differentiate it both from thirteenth-century scholasticism and modern science. She discusses in depth the theory of "double truth," the concepts of time, force, and energy, the problem of quantity or spatial extension, and the displacement of final causality by an incipient notion of the laws of nature. The insights of scholastic thinkers regarding these and other theoretical questions were, she maintains, of considerable long-term importance for the history of science: "It was perhaps at this deeper level, in the reflection about concepts, principles, and methods, that the most significant developments took place which made the thinkers of the late thirteenth and fourteenth centuries the forerunners of classical science."[9] In the final chapter, however, entitled "On the Threshold of Exact Science," she addresses the question of why, despite all their other achievements, fourteenth-century thinkers did not develop an exact mathematical physics.

The final volume in the series, *Zwischen Philosophie und Mechanik* (1958), was the first to consist wholly of new studies, although the *topics* covered are in part ones that Maier had already addressed in earlier volumes. She returned to these same questions after almost

---

9. *Metaphysische Hintergründe*, p. vii.

twenty years of research in published and unpublished sources, and consequently the studies show a surpassing depth and precision of analysis. As the title indicates, the book focuses on the science of motion in scholastic natural philosophy. Three of the seven chapters are concerned with the definition of motion, a topic Maier first investigated in an essay published in 1944. Another chapter returns to the topic of impetus, on which she had already written a long monograph. The other topics discussed include the motion of the heavens, free fall in a vacuum, and inertial motion. The overriding theme of the book is the place of scholastic mechanics in the history of physical science. Maier examines in detail the innovations late medieval thinkers made in their theory of motion and shows that although in some cases their ideas foreshadow later discoveries, on the whole scholastic mechanics represents an independent but transitional stage of development between Aristotelianism and classical physics.

The five volumes of the *Studien* all appeared between 1949 and 1958 and contain the results of two decades of amazingly productive research. Thereafter, Maier turned her attention to other projects, although two of her most important essays on the historical significance of scholastic science date from this later period. They appear in this collection of translations as chapters 5 and 7.

It is indicative of the magnitude of Anneliese Maier's achievements that for her the history of scholastic natural philosophy was only part of a broader interest in medieval intellectual history and that the *Studien* only represent part of her scholarly output. She also made major contributions to the field of codicology. At Auguste Pelzer's suggestion she undertook the task of cataloging the manuscripts of the Vatican Library's Borghese collection, which contains the remnants of the papal library at Avignon. The catalogue was published in 1952.[10] In 1957 she was chosen to catalogue the *Codices Vaticani Latini* 2118–2192, which include numerous works on natural philosophy. The completed inventory appeared in 1961.[11] In addi-

10. *Codices Burghesiani Bibliothecae Vaticanae* (Studi e Testi, 170) (Vatican City: Biblioteca apostolica vaticana, 1952).

11. *Bibliothecae Apostolicae Vaticanae codices manu scripti recensiti. Codices Vaticani Latini, Codices 2118–2192* (Vatican City: Biblioteca apostolica vaticana, 1961).

tion, she wrote many articles on other manuscripts in which she brought to light new information about their provenance, contents, and authorship. Indeed, Maier's output of essays on later thirteenth- and fourteenth-century intellectual history was prodigious, and, beginning in 1964, her collected essays appeared under the title *Ausgehendes Mittelalter*. A second volume was published in 1967.

Her researches continued unabated, and in her later years she turned her attention to the intellectual and theological milieu of the papal court at Avignon. After 1967 she was almost wholly involved in editing for publication the documents concerning the theological *cause célèbre* of the 1330s: the controversy over the beatific vision. The initial results of her research on this topic were published shortly before her death, but she was unable to see the project to completion. Decades of strenuous work had weakened her physical constitution, and on December 2, 1971, she died in Rome of influenza.[12] The products of her later research were published in 1977 as volume 3 of *Ausgehendes Mittelalter*, edited by Agostino Paravicini Bagliani. The five volumes of "Studien zur Naturphilosophie der Spätscholastik" and the three of *Ausgehendes Mittelalter*, which together comprise over 3,700 pages, remain as monuments to a prolific scholarly career of just over thirty years.

*

The history of late medieval science was a relatively new field when Anneliese Maier first became acquainted with it. The existence of flourishing schools of natural philosophy in the later Middle Ages had been almost singlehandedly discovered and publicized by the French physicist and historian Pierre Duhem (d. 1916).[13] While inquiring into the intellectual predecessors of Leonardo da Vinci, he

---

12. The most detailed obituary of Anneliese Maier appeared in *Revista di Storia della Chiesa in Italia* 20 (1972): 245–48. This notice, which was written by Jeanne Bignami Odier, is the source for many of the facts about Maier's life recounted in this introduction.

13. *Les Origines de la Statique*, 2 vols. (Paris: Hermann, 1905–06); *Études sur Léonard de Vinci*, 3 vols. (Paris: Hermann, 1906–13); *Le Système du Monde*, 10 vols. (Paris: Hermann, 1913–59).

uncovered the works of Jean Buridan (d. ca. 1358), Nicole Oresme (d. 1382), and other fourteenth-century philosophers whose mechanics and cosmology seemed strikingly modern to him. In his monumental history of cosmological theory before Copernicus, *Le Système du Monde*, he concluded, among other things, that Oresme anticipated Copernicus's theory of the diurnal rotation of the earth, Descartes's analytic geometry, and Galileo's law relating time and distance traveled in free fall.[14] He also asserted that Buridan's mechanics was the forerunner of Galileo's and that Buridan's theory of impetus foreshadowed the law of inertia of classical physics.[15] In short, he announced that the scientific revolution of the seventeenth century had actually taken place in the fourteenth century and that the late scholastic thinkers were the predecessors of Galileo and his contemporaries.

The publication of these ideas set off a major controversy over the relationship between medieval and modern science. The most effective defense of Galileo's originality was made by Alexandre Koyré in his *Études Galiléennes* (1939; reprinted Paris: Hermann, 1966), in which he argued that the discoveries of Bruno, Galileo, and Descartes constituted a break with the medieval past and were not at all based on the theories of the fourteenth-century philosophers. No general and balanced assessment of Duhem's theories, however, had yet appeared when Maier first turned her attention to scholastic natural philosophy. She first addressed the question of the relationship between scholastic thought and seventeenth-century science in her *Mechanisierung des Weltbildes* (1938), in which she cites Duhem's *Études sur Léonard de Vinci* in connection with her review of the "traditional" theory of qualities. Soon afterward, in her *Impetustheorie der Scholastik* (Vienna: Schroll, 1940), she focused on Duhem's assessment of the medieval theory of impetus, and, while recognizing the importance of his pioneering work on the subject, she rejected his conclusion that scholastic thinkers anticipated the discoveries of classical physics. This approach set the pattern for many of her early studies, which took as their starting point the correction and extension of Duhem's research.

14. *Système du Monde,* 7:534.
15. Ibid., 8:200 and 8:338.

The dominant theme of Maier's writings on medieval natural philosophy is her insistence that scholastic treatises be considered from the conceptual standpoint of their authors, not from the perspective of later scientific theories. Duhem's negligence in this regard was, in her opinion, his greatest weakness. Too often he interpreted medieval texts in a modern sense, without taking into account the context of the ideas and the metaphysical principles that gave them meaning. Maier, on the other hand, because of her thorough training in philosophy and her orientation toward questions of metaphysics, was able not only to avoid Duhem's anachronism, but also to investigate the underlying structures of scholastic thought that he had ignored. Her advantages in this regard become evident particularly in her discussions of the reasons why certain problems arose and why certain questions were asked. For Maier, an understanding of the metaphysical issues at stake in a particular problem is essential to the correct interpretation of the proposed solution. In practice, this means analyzing scholastic theories in their own terms—"from the inside out." It was this methodology, rigorously applied, that enabled Maier to establish the history of scholastic science on firm conceptual foundations.

Having undertaken a critique of Duhem, Maier was necessarily drawn into the dispute over the relationship between medieval and modern science. It is understandable, given the breadth of her scholarly vision, that she considered the question as posed by Duhem and others to be entirely too narrow. Not only was the debate over continuity restricted to a handful of issues, such as the relationship between the scholastic concept of impetus and the modern concept of inertia, but it also came to be regarded as a test of the value of scholastic natural philosophy as a whole. But, as Maier points out, the question of whether some medieval thinker formulated the "correct" solution to a given problem depends on one's point of view. To a modern physicist, both the theoretical principles and the techniques of analysis involved in the scholastic discussion of motion are "wrong." From the perspective of the natural philosopher, on the other hand, scholastic thinkers in some cases developed theories that are analogous to modern ones, although they expressed them in a different conceptual system. As with all problems of historical continuity, the question is whether one chooses to emphasize the similarities or the differences between two distinct modes of thought.

Characteristically, Maier takes a much broader approach to the question of continuity.[16] Basically, she agrees with Duhem's contention that the fourteenth-century view of nature represents a preliminary and preparatory stage in the development of modern science. She regards the history of natural philosophy from the thirteenth to the eighteenth century as the history of the gradual rejection of Aristotelianism. This rejection did not occur in a revolutionary fashion, but it also did not evolve uniformly from century to century. Instead, the displacement of Aristotle's theories occurred in two stages: the first culminated in the fourteenth century; the second, in the seventeenth. The major difference between the two stages is that the later thinkers rejected not only individual theories but also the basic principles of Aristotelian natural philosophy, something the scholastics were never able to do. Because of this change in world view, scholastic theories can at best be analogous, not equivalent, to those of classical physics. And even in the cases in which scholastic and modern explanations resemble each other, there is almost always no real physical dependency, no concrete historical continuity, but rather a correspondence solely in the realm of abstract thought.

In Maier's view, the elements of continuity must be sought not in specific theories, but in the conceptual approach to the analysis of natural phenomena. In this regard, scholastic thinkers without question went beyond Aristotle and laid the foundations for further developments. Unlike Duhem and many others, Maier always remembered that the scholastics were, first and foremost, philosophers who approached problems not from the standpoint of physical theory, but rather from that of metaphysics and ontology. In other words, they were more interested in asking what things are and how we know what they are than in asking how phenomena can be described and measured. It is not surprising, therefore, that their achievements can be found in their speculations about the basic

16. For the views summarized here see *Die Vorläufer Galileis*, pp. 1–2, and especially *Zwischen Philosophie und Mechanik*, pp. 373–82.

principles, concepts, and methods of natural philosophy. Maier's research in these areas convinced her that almost every fundamental concept later used by classical physics was discussed and given a clearer ontological definition by scholastic thinkers:[17] space, time, and mass; force and energy; motion and velocity; the "natural tendencies" of bodies; impenetrability; rarity and density; and gravity and inertia. Moreover, the scholastics made important advances in methodology, for instance in Buridan's analysis of inductive reasoning and of the laws of nature, in Bradwardine's use of the mathematical function, and in numerous discussions of probability and of infinitesimals.[18] These investigations, especially those pertaining to the theory of motion, produced results that in many cases foreshadowed later developments. Maier emphasizes, in particular, that scholastic thinkers several times came close to formulating the modern concept of inertia.

Thus, although it is true that seventeenth-century thinkers vigorously rejected the scholastic-Aristotelian metaphysics of forms and qualities and the theories derived from it, they by no means broke completely with the past. In fact, they tacitly and sometimes unconsciously continued to use many of the concepts developed by late scholastic philosophers. As Maier observes, seventeenth-century philosophers were interested above all in constructing large-scale systems and forming a new world view, and they paid far less attention to the detailed articulation of their metaphysics. Hence, although they were intent on developing a fresh approach to the study of nature, they by no means created a totally new conceptual structure. Instead, they adopted many of the concepts and ideas formulated by scholastic thinkers—particularly those of the fourteenth century—that had become standard elements of natural philosophy. To illustrate this point, Maier refers to the concept of motive force, which indeed plays a different role in classical physics

17. *Zwischen Philosophie und Mechanik,* p. 379: "Es gibt kaum einen Begriff, mit dem die Naturerkenntnis auch noch der klassischen Zeit gearbeitet hat, den die scholastischen Philosophen nicht untersucht und in ontologischer Beziehung geklärt hätten."

18. For a more detailed discussion of some of these topics see chapter 7.

than it did in scholastic mechanics. It is no longer the cause of uniform motion but of accelerated motion. But in its metaphysical content *vis motrix* remains in the seventeenth century what it was for the scholastics: an active quality that produces motion. Only the Cartesians, she notes, tried to eliminate completely the qualitative aspect of motive force. For the others, from Galileo and Gassendi to Newton and Leibniz, as for the scholastics, force causes motion, not vice versa. In the last analysis, Maier concludes, the concept of motive force that the founders of classical mechanics postulated is ontologically equivalent to the scholastic concept of impetus.[19]

It does not, however, do justice to the writings of Anneliese Maier to view them solely from the perspective of her correction of Duhem and her contributions to the problem of continuity. She in fact went far beyond Duhem in elucidating the structure and significance of scholastic natural philosophy, and in her discussions of the relationship between medieval and modern science she gives a balanced appraisal that recognizes both the achievements and limitations of late scholastic thought. Indeed, considered independently from these particular questions, her works represent the best general examination of scholastic natural philosophy available in any language. They are indispensable prerequisites to any advanced study of medieval science, especially its metaphysical foundations, theory of motion, and theory of qualities. The philosophical acuteness, knowledge of the sources, thoroughness, and dedication that characterize Anneliese Maier's scholarship are rarely found combined so advantageously in one individual; as a consequence, her studies are still unsuperseded and are likely to remain so for many years.

*

Given the importance of Anneliese Maier's works for the field of scholastic natural philosophy, it is surprising that virtually nothing

---

19. *Zwischen Philosophie und Mechanik*, p. 380: "Und letzten Endes ist diese Kraft, die die Begründer der neuen Mechanik postulieren, in ihrer ontologischen Wesensbestimmung nichts anderes als der scholastische Impetus."

she wrote is available in English.[20] Of course, specialists in the field are familiar with her writings and make use of those studies that pertain to their own particular interests. Maier's influence, therefore, has been felt largely indirectly through the writings of English-speaking scholars. Their publications have made some of her major conclusions available to a wider audience of nonspecialists interested in the development of scientific thought, but the full range of her research has by no means been represented. Generally speaking, it has been Maier's analyses of specific physical theories, such as the theory of impetus, that have attracted the attention of other scholars, while the philosophical aspects of her work have been comparatively neglected. Yet, Maier herself believed that late scholasticism made its greatest advances not in its physical theory, but in its metaphysical and methodological speculations.

Her works, particularly the "Studien zur Naturphilosophie der Spätscholastik," are listed in all the relevant bibliographies, but for various reasons they are somewhat difficult to approach. First, there is the problem of language. Maier's German, although very readable, deters all but those with a particular interest in the subject and the necessary level of proficiency in the language from acquainting themselves with her ideas. The more specialized studies also assume a good understanding of Latin, since Maier often quotes her unpublished sources at length. Throughout her works she leaves technical terms and phrases in the original Latin for the sake of precision. Moreover, the sheer volume of Maier's writings can be a deterrent simply because it is difficult to know where to begin. The order of the volumes in the *Studien* does not represent a chronological development nor necessarily one of increasing specialization, although the first volume, *Die Vorläufer Galileis,* serves in a way as an introduc-

---

20. Maier's essay " 'Ergebnisse' der spätscholastischen Naturphilosophie," which originally appeared in *Scholastik* 35 (1960): 161–88, was translated in *Philosophy Today* 5 (1961): 92–107 under the title "Philosophy of Nature at the End of the Middle Ages." This translation, however, contains serious flaws, and I have therefore retranslated the essay as chapter seven. As far as I know, nothing else by Maier is available in English.

tion to her interests and methods. Besides the *Studien*, however, there are also her essays, which often approach the same topics considered in the *Studien* in a more general and less technical fashion. Finally, little has been written about Maier's work itself, so that her purpose and orientation have to be learned along with the subject matter she considers.

This collection of essays and studies in translation attempts to alleviate some of these problems in two ways. First, it is meant to provide an introduction to Anneliese Maier's works both for those who do not read German and for those who want to become acquainted with her approach before undertaking further readings. Of the seven selections included here, four come from the *Studien* (chaps. 1–3 and 6) and focus on the content of scholastic natural philosophy, while the other three are essays published separately (chaps. 4, 5, and 7) that deal more with the historical importance of medieval science. Together they represent a rough balance between Maier's earlier and later writings and between her specialized and general studies.

The translations are further intended to provide a short but detailed introduction to the basic principles of the scholastic theories of motion and matter. These two topics are, of course, treated in a number of surveys and more advanced works in English, but unfortunately such discussions are either too elementary or too problem oriented to give the nonspecialist or the serious student a detailed theoretical understanding of the scholastic viewpoint. In fact, beyond the introductory level there is no systematic treatment in English of the cosmological assumptions of late medieval science.[21]

21. For a general introduction to the medieval world view, see C. S. Lewis, *The Discarded Image* (Cambridge: Cambridge University Press, 1964). For the twelfth century, see Brian Stock, *Myth and Science in the Twelfth Century* (Princeton: Princeton University Press, 1972). By far the best introduction to the late medieval approach to science is Nicholas Steneck, *Science and Creation in the Middle Ages* (South Bend, Ind.: University of Notre Dame Press, 1976). Steneck covers the whole spectrum of scholastic natural philosophy and thus does not examine any particular topic in depth, but his insistence that all areas of medieval science should be studied, not just those that come to the fore in the scientific revolution, is laudable. An introduc-

Maier's studies, on the other hand, are expressly concerned with the underlying principles of scholastic natural philosophy and are therefore indispensable reading for those who desire a more thorough knowledge of the subject. Five of the seven essays translated here deal with the scholastic theory of motion and address not only specific problems, such as the explanation of projectile motion, but also the metaphysical and methodological questions that concerned medieval commentators. This emphasis on mechanics reflects Maier's special interest in the topic and her belief that it was in this field that fourteenth-century thinkers made the transition from natural philosophy to natural science. The other major focus of these translations, the scholastic theory of matter, is treated in a selection in which Maier reviews the two principle explanations of the structure of material substance and the difficulties that arose in reconciling them. In contrast to scholastic mechanics, this area is one in which there is almost complete discontinuity between the medieval and modern theories, since the inadequacies of the metaphysics of form and matter helped prepare the way for the revival of atomism in the seventeenth century. The last essay is meant to complement these specialized studies by providing a general overview of the advances made by

---

tion to the theory of motion based both on Maier's studies and on more recent research is John Murdoch and Edith Sylla, "The Science of Motion" in David Lindberg, ed., *Science in the Middle Ages* (Chicago: University of Chicago Press, 1978). Another introduction can be found in Edward Grant, *Physical Science in the Middle Ages* (New York: Wiley, 1971), chap. 4. At the advanced level there is Marshall Clagett, *The Science of Mechanics in the Middle Ages* (Madison, Wis.: University of Wisconsin Press, 1959), which focuses, however, on particular problems rather than on the metaphysical background of the theory of motion. For the theory of matter, there is James Weisheipl, "The Concept of Matter in Fourteenth Century Science" in Ernan McMullin, ed., *The Concept of Matter in Greek and Medieval Philosophy* (South Bend, Ind.: University of Notre Dame Press, 1965); and Robert Multhauf, "The Science of Matter" in David Lindberg, ed., *Science in the Middle Ages* (Chicago: University of Chicago Press, 1978). An extensive bibliography of the history of medieval science can be found in Grant, *Physical Science in the Middle Ages*, pp. 91–115.

scholastic natural philosophers in metaphysics, methodology, and physical theory.

One other criterion of selection needs to be mentioned. I have tried to choose essays that I found particularly informative, perceptive, and even exciting when I first read them and that have amply repaid rereading. Generally speaking, I have tried to include whole essays or discussions rather than short excerpts so that the reader can become acquainted with Maier's presentation and style of argumentation. Technical terms and quotations in Latin have been translated into English, but the original wording is given in parentheses or in a footnote when important. My own additions and those Latin passages originally in the main body of the text are bracketed.

One:

THE NATURE OF MOTION

Most writers on medieval science take motion itself for granted and proceed immediately to describe the theories that were applied to it. In doing so, they tacitly assume (or at least allow their readers to assume) the modern idea that motion is the change of relative position of a body. For Aristotle and for scholastic thinkers, however, motion is a much broader concept that includes not only change of place (motus localis), *but other kinds of change as well. It is not, moreover, a primary concept, but one that must be defined by reference to other, more basic concepts. In Aristotelian terms, motion is the actualization of that which exists in potentiality.*

In the essay that follows, Anneliese Maier examines the scholastic response to one of the most difficult problems resulting from this definition of motion, the question of what category motion itself belongs in. The essay is one of the earliest products of her researches into scholastic natural philosophy and was first published in 1944 as "Die scholastische Wesensbestimmung der Bewegung" (Angelicum *21 [1944]:97–111). It was reprinted as the first chapter of* Die Vorläufer Galileis *(Rome: Edizioni di Storia e Letteratura, 1949), and this text is the one translated here. It was reprinted again with supplementary comments in the second edition of* Die Vorläufer Galileis *(Rome: Edizioni di Storia e Letteratura, 1962). Meanwhile, Maier reexam-*

ined the whole question of the definition of motion in much greater detail in the first three chapters of Zwischen Philosophie und Mechanik *(Rome: Edizioni di Storia e Letteratura, 1958), in which she made use of numerous manuscript sources not known to her in 1944. The basic outlines of her analysis, however, did not change. This essay, then, provides an introduction to the scholastic-Aristotelian concept of motion that can be supplemented, for those who desire a more detailed discussion, by the material presented in* Zwischen Philosophie und Mechanik.

The first and foremost problem of scholastic physics is the concept of motion. Its importance to scholastic thinking is far greater than the corresponding concept of motion in Galilean and post-Galilean mechanics, and it in fact amounts to a generalized concept of physical process. Scholastic-Aristotelian philosophy conceives of motion as the transition from potentiality to actuality or vice versa, and it therefore occurs in every formal category in which the distinction between actual and potential being can be made. According to Aristotle, there are four such categories: substance, quantity, quality, and place.[1] Thus, the generalized concept of motion includes (1) *generatio* and *corruptio,* that is, the creation and dissolution of substances; (2) increase or decrease in quantity, which can occur either with an increase or decrease in material (*augmentatio* and *diminutio* in the strict sense, which only happen in living beings) or simply with an increase or decrease in volume without any gain or loss of material *(rarefactio* and *condensatio);*[2] (3) qualitative change or *alteratio,* of which the most important special case is the phenomenon of increase or decrease of intensity *(intensio* and *remissio);* and (4) change of place *(motus localis),* which Aristotle himself characterized as the most basic and important kind of motion.

1. Aristotle, *Praedicamenta,* cap. 14; *Physica* III, cap. 1; and elsewhere.
2. Aristotle's remarks on the latter case, however, are not consistent, and sometimes they are used to support the view that *rarefactio* and *condensatio* are qualitative changes. But the other interpretation predominates and can be attributed to Aristotle with as much or even greater justification.

A more precise definition of the concept of motion requires a further qualification that Aristotle himself proposed[3] and that won nearly universal acceptance among scholastic thinkers. Motion in the true, strict sense is not simply the process of transition from potentiality to actuality or vice versa, but rather a transition that takes place gradually and in successive stages, not suddenly and in one jump. A change of state that does not proceed gradually is termed a *mutatio* and is distinguished from motion in the strict sense. Scholastic thinkers for the most part regarded the phenomena of *generatio* and *corruptio* as examples of *mutatio:* the actualization of a substantial form in matter and its relapse back into the potency of the matter are considered to be processes that happen abruptly and instantaneously, not by degrees. Hence generation and corruption were either not classified as motion or only regarded as motion in the loose sense of the word.

Succession is thus an essential element in the concept of motion. It is conceived of as the fundamental and unique ordering into prior and posterior states that belongs implicitly to the concept of motion; it is not, in principle, identified with temporal progression. Aristotle and the scholastic thinkers regarded time as something derived from motion; it is the "measure of motion with respect to prior and posterior" *(mensura motus secundum prius et posterius)*. Time makes explicit the element of succession contained in the phenomenon of motion. This idea, although very foreign to modern thinkers, is of fundamental importance to the theory of motion developed in high and late scholasticism.

Motion is thus the acquisition or loss, in successive stages, of a categorical attribute, a so-called "perfection"; it is, in other words, a continual change of state *(aliter et aliter se habere)* with respect to one of the three categories of quantity, quality, or place. The question now arises, In which category does motion itself belong? Is it essentially identical with the "perfection" ultimately acquired; that is, does motion itself belong in the same category in which the change takes place? Or does motion represent a special "passion" *(passio)* all by itself? Since both solutions can be supported by pas-

3. Aristotle, *Physica* V, cap. 1–2; *Metaphysica* X, cap. 12; and elsewhere.

sages in Aristotle,[4] the correct answer became a matter for dispute. Among scholastic thinkers the question was generally posed in the form of a choice between two unique alternatives: is motion a *forma fluens* or a *fluxus formae?*

This problem occupied a position of considerable importance in scholastic natural philosophy because of its unusual nature. Not only did the answer to the question completely determine the concept of motion with all its implications, but the formulation of the problem itself became the object of considerable discussion. This situation arose because very early on the actual source of the antithesis was forgotten. The concepts of *forma fluens* and *fluxus formae* were usually thought to derive from a passage in Averroes[5] that, although it does contain a corresponding distinction, does not in fact employ the two ideas. Both were foreign to the conceptual outlook of scholasticism.[6] Occasionally someone would assert that "this distinction was never made by the Commentator"[7] and reject it as meaningless. Here and there an author attributed the antithesis to Avicenna. The Latin translation of Avicenna's *Physics,* the *Sufficientia,* does, in fact, contain a passage that conveys the sense of the distinction[8] without, however, introducing the two concepts in question.

The actual originator of this formulation of the problem, which attracted so much attention and generated so much controversy, was Albertus Magnus. In a chapter of his commentary on the *Physics,*[9] Albert discusses the question, "Whether motion is in the cate-

4. The first one by *Physica* III, cap. 1, *Metaphysica* X, cap. 9; the other by *Praedicamenta,* cap. 9.

5. Averroes, *Physica* III, comm. 4 (*Opera* [Venice, 1550], vol. 4).

6. By their nature, forms are supposed to be unchangeable. A frequently cited passage from the *Liber sex principiorum* says "form is that which consists in a simple and invariable essence" (*forma est simplici et invariabili essentia consistens*). A form that flows (*forma fluens*) or the flux of a form (*fluxus formae*) is thus, strictly speaking, a contradiction in terms.

7. For instance, Petrus Aureoli (*Sent.* II, dist. 1, qu. 3, art. I [Rome, 1596–1605]). [*Ista distinctio nunquam fuit Commentatoris.*]

8. Avicenna, *Sufficientia* II, cap. 1–2 (Venice, 1508).

9. Albertus Magnus, *Physica* III, tract. I, cap. 3 (*Opera,* ed. Borgnet, vol. 3 [Paris, 1890]).

gories and how it is in them." His basic approach is to follow Averroes, but since Averroes's discussion appeared obscure and questionable to him, Albert attempts to clarify and sharpen it. He proceeds to list and analyze the theories of motion advocated by a variety of earlier commentators on Aristotle, a task for which he claims Avicenna as his predecessor.[10] In the process Albert introduces the two concepts that he then uses as aids in interpreting Averroes's commentary. This explains why the distinction between *forma fluens* and *fluxus formae* was later attributed to Averroes by some commentators and to Avicenna by others.

Averroes himself formulates the problem as follows.[11] On the one hand, motion differs from the "perfection" attained as a result of the motion only in degree, not in essence. Viewed from this standpoint, motion belongs in the same category as the goal to which it is directed, since motion is nothing more than the gradual creation of the "perfection" in question.[12] If, on the other hand, one considers motion to be the process by which the "perfection" is attained, then it is a genus unto itself, since the "way to the thing" *(via ad rem)* is different from the "thing" itself. Considered in this fashion, motion actually represents a special category. Averroes adds that the second idea is more renowned, but the first is more correct.[13]

It is this passage that Albert attempts to interpret and clarify by investigating various approaches to the conceptualization of motion. As mentioned, he indicates explicitly that he is following Avicenna, although in truth his discussion is more a free paraphrase of Avicenna than a recapitulation of the frequently obscure chapters of the *Sufficientia*.

Albert begins the discussion by observing that motion can be considered from three different angles. First, it can be considered

10. "But because Averroes's solution is obscure and questionable, before we inquire into it let us touch on all the other opinions of the Peripatetics concerning the nature of motion; Avicenna appears to have touched on them before us in the *Sufficientia.*"

11. Averroes, *Physica* III, comm. 4.

12. "For motion is nothing other than the generation of one part after another of the perfection toward which the motion tends."

13. *Et iste modus est famosior, ille autem est verior.*

with reference to the mover; from this perspective, motion belongs in the category of action *(actio)*. Second, it can be considered with reference to the thing moved; in this case, motion must be classified with things acted upon *(passiones)*. Aristotle, he says, takes this view in the *Praedicamenta*. Finally, motion can be considered with reference to the goal of the motion (the *finis et terminus motus*); from this standpoint, it appears to be the "flow of some being toward that which is the goal of the motion" *(fluxus alicuius entis in id quod est terminus motus)*. Thus, the process of becoming black *(nigrescere)*, for example, is a "flow toward blackness" *(fluxus in nigredinem)*; an increase in quantity *(augmentatio)* is a "flow to the quantity attained" *(fluxus ad perfectam quantitatem)*; and local motion is a "flow to a place" *(fluxus ubi)*.

Those who adopt this last point of view, he continues, fall into two classes. Some assert that this flow does not differ from the goal at which the motion comes to a halt in species or in essence *(differentia specifica sive per essentiam)*, but only in its mode of being *(per esse tantum)*: motion represents "being in flux" *(esse in fluxu)*, while the ultimate goal represents "being at rest" *(esse in quiete)*. This idea, which Averroes seems to have adopted, puts motion itself in the category in which the change takes place. The process of becoming black *(nigrescere)* is a "transient or flowing blackness" *(nigredo pertransiens sive fluens)*, and upward motion *(ascendere)* is a "flowing of place" *(ubi fluens)*.

Others, however, assert that the flow of being *(fluxus entis)* that constitutes motion is something different from the goal in both species and essence. Thus, the process of becoming black differs in essence and specific difference from blackness and is therefore neither a quality nor the species of a quality. Motion, in short, belongs to a category different from the goal it attains. It is a separate and distinct flowing *(fluxus)* and is not simply identical with the form in a state of flux *(forma in fluxu)* or with the being that flows *(ens fluens)*.

This *fluxus formae*, moreover, can itself be conceived in two ways. One can argue that it does not belong in any known category and is instead only a "process leading to the categorical result" *(via ad rem praedicamenti)* or a "principle leading to it" *(principium ad ipsam)*.

According to Albert, Avicenna advocated this solution. Or, one can consider motion as such to be a category by itself *(praedicamentum per se)* that can be predicated in exactly the same sense *(univoce)* of all the various kinds of motion. This approach treats the different kinds of motion as species subsumed, as it were, under the generic concept of "motion." Albert rejects this theory, however, calling it an "unsound opinion" *(sententia debilis)*, because the various types of motion do not have anything in common univocally *(secundum univocationem)* and therefore cannot be considered to be species of an overriding genus.

Albert thus selects five of the most famous theories of motion from among the numerous possibilities, but eliminates the last of these immediately. He then conducts a detailed examination of the arguments for and against the first two explanations and concludes that they too must be rejected. There is a difference between considering motion with reference to the mover that causes it and simply with reference to the being that resides in the moving object *(secundum esse quod habet in mobili)*. Only the latter approach permits us to comprehend the real essence of motion. Albert uses this distinction to exclude the first interpretation: in its essence, motion is at most the effect of an applied action *(actionis agentis effectus)*, not the action itself. The second theory, that motion is "being acted on," is also incorrect for the same reason, since here again the reference to the cause of the motion comes into play. At most it can be said that "there is passion in motion" *(in motu est passio)*, since all motion presupposes the action of a mover on the object moved. But it cannot be said that "motion is passion" *(motus est passio)*.

Thus, the only theories still under consideration for the true definition of motion are the third and fourth ones, those of Averroes and Avicenna, respectively. Albert characterizes the two alternatives with the terms *forma fluens* and *fluxus formae*.

Albert adopts Averroes's solution without, however, completely excluding Avicenna's. In his opinion, motion belongs in the category in which the change takes place, is identical in essence with the goal it attains, and differs from the goal not in essence but only in its mode of being *(secundum esse)*. Motion represents being in flux *(esse in fluxu),* while the goal represents being at rest *(esse in quiete).* [14]

Nevertheless, Albert does not mean to reject Avicenna's explanation entirely. The idea that motion as such is a flowing that does not belong to any genus, but is only the way to a genus *(via ad genus),* is partially correct, since categories can only contain things that exist *(entia):* "motion, however, because of its imperfection is not strictly speaking something that exists, but pertains to something that exists" *(motus autem propter sui imperfectionem non est ens proprie loquendo, sed est entis).* To this extent Avicenna's theory contains a kernel of truth. The real solution to the problem, however, is the other one, which Albert considers to be Averroes's true opinion: motion and its goal *(terminus motus)* are identical in essence. Motion is the same as the form it attains, but it represents that form in a state of flux *(forma fluens),* not in a state of rest *(forma quiescens).*

These concepts, which soon achieved general currency in the scholastic philosophy of Albert's successors, have attracted considerable attention in recent years, although they have not always been understood correctly. [15] The concept of *forma fluens* in particular has occasionally been the subject of some peculiar interpretations. These purport to show that the scholastics opposed to the fixed, unchanging forms of Greek philosophy the notion of "flowing forms" and that from these forms they could have developed the

---

14. Albert elucidates this idea with the following example:

> If we imagine that a flowing point makes a line and that its flowing comes to an end at some point where it stops, then it is true that the endpoint of the line made by the flowing point is internal and essential to the line; and we cannot say that the endpoint is different in essence from the point that flows; but its being is that of an endpoint, not that of a point which flows. The situation is, however, in every respect similar in qualitative flowing and its termination and in quantitative flowing and its termination, and thus in other cases. Therefore motion and its endpoint are of the same [essence], and thus it is clear that motion is in the same category as its endpoint.

15. Especially in connection with Duhem's essay "Le mouvement absolu et le mouvement relatif," *Revue de philosophie* VII-IX, 1907–1909.

modern theory of mathematical functions and even Newton's method of fluxions.

This is totally out of the question. Albertus Magnus himself excluded this interpretation with his statement that quiescent form and flowing form differ only in their mode of being, not in their essence. In other words, the difference is not in the form itself, but in the participation of the subject in the form. Forms themselves are by nature unchangeable. The flowing results from the successive realization in a subject of different species of the same genus (such as color or size) or of different degrees within the same species (as in the case of an increase or decrease in intensity). It is not the form that flows, but rather its mode of being, that is, its realization as something that inheres in a subject.[16]

This is the sense in which Albert considers motion to be a *forma fluens*, and his solution to the problem remained standard in scholastic philosophy until the 1420s. It was almost always argued that motion and its goal, or, in other words, motion and the form acquired as a result of it, coincide.[17] Motion does not differ from the form with respect to which *(secundum quam)* it occurs; motion and its goal are not only alike in essence, they are actually identical. In this theory, local motion is equated with place, qualitative change with the quality in question, and quantitative change with the quantity that changes.

The concept is not as absurd as it appears to be at first glance, since the scholastics, as was mentioned earlier, incorporated the idea of succession into their concept of motion. Thus for them the equation of motion and its goal *(terminus)* implies immediately and tacitly that motion is equivalent to a succession of distinct, temporary "goals" *(termini)*.

16. Or, if one considers generation and corruption to be motion, as Albert does in this discussion, the realization of form in matter.

17. Hervaeus Natalis (*Sent.* I, dist. 17, qu. 4 [Venice, 1505]) observes: "The endpoint of the motion, which is the form acquired as a result of the motion, is not asserted to be different in a real sense from the motion. For it is commonly maintained that the form acquired as a result of a motion and the motion [itself] are identical in a real sense." William of Alnwick formulates this idea (which he himself rejects; see footnote 20) in the following manner: "Therefore motion is more correctly a *forma fluens* than a *fluxus formae*."

One of the peculiarities of scholastic thought that also manifests itself in other contexts is that the temporal element is suppressed in the analysis of concepts or, rather, that it is not presented explicitly. It is, of course, taken into account implicitly, but in general no attempt is made to discuss the topic directly. The rationale for this varies from case to case, but the real reason is always the same: scholastic-Aristotelian philosophy was not able to comprehend non-static, successive phenomena and classify them in terms of its system of categories. The solution to this difficulty would have been to regard *fluxus formae* as a special category, but this option was expressly rejected by scholasticism as a whole and by Albertus Magnus in particular.

To continue, when motion occurs only one intermediate "goal" or state *(terminus)* is realized at a time, never several simultaneously. Motion is therefore actually identical at each particular moment with the state *(terminus)* attained in that moment, and in general motion is equal to the sum of all the states occupied *(termini motus)*—or to *terminus motus* considered as a genus—given that the successive character of the states is implicitly understood. Thus the ontological definition of motion requires only the object that moves, the *termini motus* (in the case of local motion, for instance, the collection of places occupied), and the fact that the various *termini* are traversed in succession. This, however, is nothing other than William of Ockham's famous (and infamous) definition of motion.

We see, therefore, that Ockham did not, as is usually thought, invent this theory. It was well known and had been almost universally accepted for some time. Ockham's contribution, the essential element that makes his theory of motion different, lies in the nominalistic conclusions that he draws from the standard conception. In discussing the ontological description of motion, Ockham distinguishes carefully between the real and nominal definitions, that is, between considering the matter *de re* (with regard to the thing itself) and *de modo loquendi* (with regard to how we talk about it).[18] The real definition simply coincides with the standard scholastic conception

18. Ockham, *Philosophia naturalis* (= *Summulae in libros Physicorum Aristotelis)*, pars III, cap. 2–7 (Rome, 1637); *Sent.* II, qu. 9 (Lyon, 1495); and elsewhere.

of motion.[19] Motion is identical with the moving object that occupies different places successively (or, to phrase it negatively, never occupies more than one place at a time). In the other categories, it is identical with the subject that exhibits different qualities or different quantities successively. Motion is not a concrete or objective element distinct from the *res permanentes*, that is, from the moving object and the states it occupies *(termini motus)*. Like all scholastics, Ockham takes into account the notion of succession implicitly without differentiating it as an independent categorical element in the concept of motion. Past and future have no extramental reality; they exist only in the soul. What is real in motion is the configuration attained at each present moment, and this configuration only involves the moving object and the momentary *terminus*.

This analysis, which in no way differs from the usual scholastic interpretation of motion, provides the starting point for the nominal definition that leads to a complete nominalization. If motion is not something distinct from the moving object and the states it occupies, then nothing real corresponds to the concept of motion; it is merely a word or label. To say that something is in motion is a way of expressing the idea that it does not occupy two places simultaneously or that it does not have different qualities at the same time. But abstract concepts such as motion and mutation do not have any objective referents. They are merely superfluous and dispensable names or words that were created for the sake of elegance in discourse rather than from necessity *(magis inventa sunt propter venustatem eloquii quam propter necessitatem)* and that do not stand for anything external to the soul *(res extra animam)*. This conclusion, and it alone, represents what is unusual in Ockham's theory of motion. In all other respects he adhered to the predominant scholastic interpretation.

19. "And I say that, when something is moved, it suffices that the moving object acquire something continuously, without interruption or rest, by continuous parts that succeed one after another; or that it lose something either continuously and successively or by parts; just as, . . . in the case of local motion, it suffices that it acquire one place after another continuously without stopping, so that it is in different places successively without stopping" *(Philosophia naturalis*, pars III, cap. 6).

Ockham's nominalistic approach to the concept of motion was, on the whole, more often rejected than accepted by fourteenth-century natural philosophers, and its direct influence was less important than its indirect effect in stimulating opposition. One of the most important results was that the problem of motion itself once again became a topic for discussion, and the old question of *forma fluens* or *fluxus formae* was revived in a new and much more precise form. Confronted with the nominalistic analysis, scholastic thinkers asked whether motion can in fact be adequately defined in terms of the moving object, on the one hand, and the *termini* or the form with respect to which the motion occurs, on the other. Is not motion rather something real and external to the soul, a flux that somehow exists and is distinct from the moving object and the states it acquires?

Such considerations led to a new and subtle reformulation of the question. Motion continued to be regarded as a *forma fluens* in at least one respect, namely, in the material sense *(secundum materiam)*. Considered from this standpoint, it is in fact identical with the *termini* that succeed one another. But the question now arose, Should some further categorical element be postulated in addition, some kind of flux that constitutes the true essence of the reality we call motion? The new approach was less concerned with choosing between *forma fluens* and *fluxus formae* than with understanding how both *forma fluens* and *fluxus formae* may be involved.

Doubts of this kind began to appear as early as the 1420s among a variety of Scotists, who decided in favor of *fluxus formae*.[20] But

20. Francis of Meyronnes, for example, asks in his commentary on the *Sentences* composed in 1320–21 (lib. II, dist. 14, qu. 9 [Venice, 1520]): "But what is motion?" and he replies: "It is said that [motion is] not a *forma fluens* but a *fluxus formae,* which is nothing other than the succession of form *(successio formae)."* William of Alnwick treats the question in an especially clear and penetrating manner in one of the *questiones* that he debated in Bologna in 1323: "Whether motion is of the same genus as its endpoint" *(Utrum motus sit de genere termini ad quem* in Ms. Vat. Pal. lat. 1805, fol. 148–51). Here he concludes: "For motion is in a formal sense a certain successive flux of the form flowing from one endpoint to the other." *(Motus enim est formaliter fluxus quidam successivus formae fluentis a termino in terminum.)* He regards

these efforts remained isolated at first and did not lead to a unified theory of motion. Such an analysis only emerged in the natural philosophy of the Parisian school of "terminists," that is, in the "new physics" taught by Jean Buridan and his students and followers. Here, as elsewhere, Ockham's theory of motion did not find ready acceptance, but instead stimulated its opponents to ask whether motion might indeed be something real and distinct from the object and its states or, in other words, whether another flux ought to be postulated in conjunction with the *forma fluens*.

The first step in answering this question was to sharpen the definition of the problem. Buridan[21] and his successors (especially Albert of Saxony,[22] who saw the problem clearly and made precise distinctions) began by distinguishing local motion from all other kinds. They recognized correctly that motion with respect to place is unlike alteration, for instance, in that the goal of the motion is not a "perfection" that inheres in the moving object, but rather an external disposition. In his analysis of qualitative change, Buridan adheres in every respect to the traditional (and Ockhamistic) conception. Motion in this case is nothing more than the *forma fluens* and is thus essentially identical with the goal of the motion; no flux distinct from the subject and the quality that changes needs to be postulated. But Buridan completely rejects the corresponding explanation for local motion. Here motion and its goal cannot coincide, since motion is in the moving object subjectively, while place is not *(motus est subiective in mobili, locus autem non)*.

Local motion is instead something inherent in the moving object that defies further specification. This answer can be illustrated and substantiated by considering an unusual problem that was already the object of considerable discussion in the thirteenth century.

---

continuous succession as the characteristic feature and thus arrives at the following more precise definition: "I say therefore that motion, since it is the flux of a form conjointly with time *(fluxus formae coniunctus cum tempore)*, is in its formal sense essentially successive quantity *(quantitas successiva)*." Thus motion is formally and essentially "in the genus quantity."

21. Buridan, *Physica* III, qu. 2, qu. 6–9 (Paris, 1509).

22. Albert of Saxony, *Physica* III, qu. 4–8 (Venice, 1504).

Within the conceptual framework of scholasticism it is possible to imagine a case in which local motion occurs without reference to place and therefore does not involve constant change of position and cannot be regarded as "flowing place" *(ubi fluens)*. Such would be the motion of the outermost sphere of the heavens, which, according to the scholastic-Aristotelian theory of space, is no longer "in place" *(in loco)*,[23] but can nevertheless be set in motion by God's omnipotence.[24] (The condemnations of 1277 excluded the opposite view.) Obviously, in this case motion must be something different from the thing moved and the place, since the place does not come into consideration at all.[25] Instead, to be moved *(moveri)* is "to be continually intrinsically different" *(intrinsece aliter et aliter se ha-*

---

23. In Aristotle's view, place is of course the *ultimum continentis*, that is, the inner surface of the surrounding substance. But no such thing exists for the outermost sphere of the heavens; it contains but is not itself contained.

24. The universe is conceived to be set in motion as a whole, reduced as it were to a single compact mass, so that no motion of its individual parts relative either to each other or to some fixed center comes into consideration.

25. Of course, the obvious thought also occurred to scholastic philosophers that if God could set the entire universe in motion, he could just as well create empty space outside of it for this motion to take place in. Richard of Mediavilla, for example, makes this clear with his straightforward remark that even God could not effect motion of this kind without there being some such space *(Sent.* II, dist. 14, art. III, qu. 3). Buridan's followers likewise expressed the idea that the motion of the universe as a whole presupposes the notion of empty space surrounding it, although they did so in the context of other problems, as in Nicole Oresme's *Traité du ciel et du monde,* livre II, chap. 8, Ms. Paris Bibl. Nat. fonds franc. 1083, fol. 56v. [Now see Nicole Oresme, *Le Livre du ciel et du monde,* ed. A. D. Menut and A. J. Denomy, trans. A. D. Menut (Madison, Wis.: University of Wisconsin Press, 1968)]; cf. E. Borchert, "Die Lehre von der Bewegung bei Nicolaus Oresme," in *Beiträge zur Geschichte der Philosophie und Theologie des Mittelalters,* XXXI, 3, p. 47 ff. In discussing the question of the nature of motion, however, they intentionally avoided this possibility since their purpose was to demonstrate that local motion can occur without place and thus that motion must be some factor different from the place and the moving object.

34

bere).[26] Thus, local motion itself is by no means only a name, but rather something real that inheres in the moving object and is distinct from it.[27] It is a pure successiveness *(res pure successive)* or flux that is not reducible to other categories and must simply be affirmed in its uniqueness.[28] This solution to the problem also pro-

26. Duns Scotus had in fact already arrived at a similar solution (although expressed in different terminology) that, however, he expressly limited to the motion of the outermost sphere of the heavens. For him motion is essentially a *forma fluens* in the usual sense we described earlier (cf. for example *Opus Oxoniense* I, dist. 2, qu. 7). But this interpretation, of course, fails when applied to the possible motion of the outermost heavens. Scotus therefore concludes that in this case (and only in this case!) the *forma fluens* with respect to which there is *per se* circular motion is a purely absolute form *(forma mere absoluta),* independent of the place and the object ("without reference either to what contains or what is contained"—*Quodlibeta,* qu. 11). And this absolute *forma fluens* is exactly equivalent to what later philosophers have in mind when they speak of *fluxus formae* or similar ideas. But, as we said, Scotus admits this solution only for the imaginary case of the motion of the outermost heavens and draws no conclusions from this example about the nature of motion as such, something which later thinkers did do. For all other earthly and celestial motions he adheres to the traditional concept of *forma fluens* as a "form with respect to which there is a flowing." This vagueness in his terminology gave rise to numerous misunderstandings and occasionally caused a theory of motion to be attributed to him that was the opposite of the one he actually held.

27. This notion is not to be interpreted in a dynamic sense as Michalski did in "Les courants critiques et sceptiques dans la philosophie du XIVe siècle," *Bulletin de l'académie polonaise des sciences et des lettres,* Classe d'histoire et de philosophie, année 1925, p. 242. He mistakenly took the concept *dispositio,* which for Buridan means simply the *forma fluens* ("form or *dispositio* relative to which the moving object is continually different before and after") to mean a motive force and then went on to draw further conclusions.

28. Albert of Saxony (*Physica* III, qu. 7) summarizes this theory in the following series of conclusions: "The first conclusion is that the world is not said to be moved because it is continually different with respect to something extrinsic" and also not (second conclusion) "because it is continually different in relation to something extrinsic, if there were such a

vides us with an example of the transition from *cognitio propter quid* to *cognitio quia,* that is, from metaphysical explanation to phenomenological description, which occurs everywhere in the fourteenth century. Motion is that aspect of a moving body that is real, empirically ascertainable, and incapable of further ontological analysis; it is distinct from the moving object and from place; it cannot be explained more fully, but it does not need to be.

This definition of motion played a fairly important role in fourteenth-century natural philosophy. It had, moreover, considerable practical effect on physics proper, which was gradually beginning to free itself from philosophy. On the whole, late scholastic philosophers took exactly the same approach to concrete physical questions

---

thing" (i.e., with respect to some possibly existing space outside the world); "third, that the world is said to be moved because it is continually intrinsically different [*continue se habet aliter et aliter intrinsece*]; fourth, this intrinsicness is not the moving object, although it would be something inherent in it; fifth, this intrinsicness relative to which the moving object is continually different is the motion itself or the flux [*fluxus*]; sixth, that such motion is a thing distinct from the moving object; seventh, in every object in local motion . . . it is necessary to conceive a flux or a motion inherent in the object which is acquired in successive stages by the object." Also, in treating the question (no. 6) "Whether according to Aristotle and his Commentator it is necessary in the case of local motion that there be something else, that is, a flux distinct from the object and the place," Albert first makes the following observation: "This question can perhaps have different answers depending on whether Aristotle and the Commentator or the real truth is accepted." In the discussion that follows he supports the second alternative with the conclusions cited above. First, however, Albert explains that the true interpretation of Aristotle's and Averroes's theory of motion is still a matter for dispute, but that in his opinion their interpretation is the following: "when something is moved it is necessary and sufficient that there be an object, a place, and a mover. Nevertheless these are not [understood] absolutely, rather [it is understood] that the object is continuously and successively in different places [*continue et successive sit in alio et alio loco*], assuming the immobility of place . . . nor is some additional flux necessary." Although this is not an exact restatement of the Aristotelian theory, it is in any case a precise formulation fo the usual theory of *forma fluens.*

36

as physical scientists of every age. When they began to feel uneasy with their exceedingly abstract philosophical concepts they tacitly reverted to and worked with the naive, empirical concepts of pre-scientific thinking. This explains why they analyzed problems of kinetics not in terms of *forma fluens* and the Aristotelian definitions of space and time, but rather in terms of a purely descriptive defini-tion of local motion that viewed it simply as progressive change of place.[29] This change of place, moreover, was conceived not in rela-tion to a containing surface *(ultimum continentis)* in the Aristotelian sense, but rather in relation to the empirical space of practical experience, the same space that Galileo had in mind and that New-ton finally officially incorporated into physics as "absolute space."[30] The same thing can be said about the scholastic philosophers' no-tion of time.[31]

Alongside these empirical concepts, however, one encounters an-other interpretation of local motion in the fourteenth century that

29. Johannes Canonicus (*Physica* VI, qu. 1, art. 1 [Venice, 1492]) defines it quite simply: "To be moved locally is nothing more than to vary the position which something has in space." *(Nihil aliud est moveri localiter quam variare suum situm quem habet in loco.)*

30. When, however, late scholastic thinkers attempt to describe explicitly this concept of space, which was for them usually something implicit, the result is still entirely nonphysical and very medieval: "And thus outside the heavens there is an empty, incorporeal space which is different from full and corporeal space, just as the duration called eternity is different from temporal duration, even if it were perpetual. . . . Likewise this space men-tioned above is infinite and indivisible and is the immensity of God and is God Himself, just as the duration of God called eternity is infinite and indivisible and God Himself." This is the explanation offered by Nicole Oresme, who was the only philosopher who explicitly recognized and described this space (*Traité*, livre I, chap. 24; fol. 21v [Menut and Denomy, p. 176, ll. 307–14]).

31. Besides so-called "intrinsic time" *(tempus intrinsecum)*, which is the measure of each individual motion, high scholastic thinkers had already conceived of an "extrinsic time" *(tempus extrinsecum)*, which is the measure of the motion of the outermost heavens. This is already very close to the concept of absolute time in the Newtonian sense.

incorporates features of the theory of *fluxus formae*. In it, local motion is regarded as an inherent attribute of the moving object, a sort of qualitative factor whose nature admittedly remains somewhat indefinite and unclear.[32] If, however, late scholastic thinkers had taken a step further in this direction, if they had only tried to formulate this unusual idea more precisely and give it conceptual definition, they might have arrived at something analogous to the modern law of inertia. Motion might have been conceived as a kind of attribute or condition—an independent accident of the moving object—that continues to exist by itself once it has been imparted to the object and that does not need to be maintained by a continually acting motive force, as Aristotelian philosophy demands. As I have said, all that was required was a small step further in this same direction, and the inventors of the "new physics" of the fourteenth century would have discovered this fundamental law of modern mechanics. But they did not take this step.

The analogy between motion and inherent qualities did undergo further development, but in another direction involving the conceptual analysis of velocity. On the one hand, velocity can be viewed as the distance covered in a specified time. This notion accords well not only with the empirical perception of motion, but also with the general definition of *velocitas*. On the other hand, velocity can be viewed in the context of the theory of qualities as the intensity of motion.

What is important here is that under certain circumstances local motion can be thought of as a qualitative attribute of variable intensity. It was this theory of motion that, to a great extent, dominated fourteenth-century physics and gave it the characteristic features that distinguished it so fundamentally from modern physics. The

---

32. One finds an unusual fusion of both points of view in Nicole Oresme ... [whose writings] reveal a surprising insight into the relativity of motion (*Traité*, livre II, chap. 8; fol. 57 [Menut and Denomy, pp. 364, 370, and 372]). ... Oresme's commentary on the *Physics*, in which he presumably discussed the problem of a superadded flux directly, is not preserved. Thus we are forced to infer his views on the nature of motion from incidental comments which actually pertain to other problems.

theory admittedly suffered from numerous difficulties and led to many errors, but it also made possible some real discoveries. It was the point of departure for what was undoubtedly the most original achievement of the fourteenth century—Nicole Oresme's method of graphical representation. Although Oresme's technique did not, as was for a long time supposed, anticipate Descartes' analytic geometry, it did lead to some surprisingly correct insights into the relationship between velocity and distance and into other problems. And these insights proceeded directly from that novel definition of motion that in turn derived from Albertus Magnus' question, *forma fluens* or *fluxus formae?*

Two:

CAUSES, FORCES, AND
RESISTANCE

Scholastic natural philosophy and modern physics differ not only in how they define the nature of motion, but also in their assumptions about the relationship between motive forces and the motions they produce. Only by gaining a clear understanding of these differences can a modern observer correctly evaluate the problems scholastic thinkers encountered and the solutions they proposed and thus avoid anachronistic interpretations. In the following essay Anneliese Maier gives a brief but remarkably detailed introduction to the principles of scholastic dynamics. In part I she discusses the scholastic idea of causation, the kinds of motive forces recognized, and the rules governing their operation. She then shows how two important natural phenomena, gravitational motion and projectile motion, presented major difficulties for this theoretical approach and ultimately caused scholastic thinkers to introduce significant innovations into their fundamentally Aristotelian conceptual system. Part II examines the equally important topic of the role resistance played in the scholastic theory of motion.

The selection translated here first appeared as chapter 3 ("Ursachen und Kräfte") of Die Vorläufer Galileis *(Rome: Edizioni di Storia e Letteratura, 1949), pp. 53–72. I have omitted the third part of the original chapter (pp. 73–78), which contains a brief investigation of the scholastic problem of action and reaction. Maier considers the problem of gravitation in much greater detail in Part II ("Das Problem der Gravitation") of* An der Grenze von Scholastik und Naturwissenschaft *(Essen: Essener Verlagsanstalt, 1943; 2d ed. Rome: Edizioni di Storia e Letteratura, 1952). The theory of impetus is examined in chapters 4 and 5 below.*

I

Following Aristotle, scholastic thinkers distinguished four kinds of cause: material, formal, final, and efficient. The material cause, although absolutely necessary, plays only a passive role in causation, and it presented no difficulties for scholastic physics. The same was true for the formal cause. In later centuries polemicists exaggerated and distorted the role of form as an active principle as part of their attacks on scholastic-Aristotelian natural philosophy. In reality, the situation was much simpler than the critics made it out to be. The formal cause was never treated as an active principle that makes things happen or changes existing conditions. Its function was merely to account for a state or mode of being. The fact, for instance, that a particular composite is a stone means that the substantial form of stoneness *(lapideitas)* is its formal cause. Likewise, an object is white insofar as it participates in whiteness *(albedo)*. But *albedo* is not the cause of the object's becoming white in the first place. To explain that process there has to be an efficient cause, that is, a real physical agent. Critics frequently forgot or intentionally ignored this point when they charged scholastic thinkers with trying to explain nature by using substantial and accidental forms. Formal cause has its place in the metaphysical and ontological interpretation of the world, but not in physical and dynamic explanations of nature. There are indeed a few accidental forms that can also function as efficient causes, but they operate as active principles only insofar as they are efficient causes, not by virtue of their being formal causes. They are discussed later in the chapter.

Final cause likewise by no means played the leading role in scholastic natural philosophy that later critics attributed to it in their attacks. The notion that every agent acts toward some end *(omne agens agit propter finem)* was indeed accepted as a fundamental principle, but final causes, like formal causes, were not regarded as active agents for the purpose of explaining natural phenomena. Instead, it was a basic axiom of scholastic metaphysics and natural philosophy that every final cause presupposes a corresponding efficient cause through which it is realized.

Consequently, the scholastic theory of nature was as thoroughly grounded in efficient causality as is modern physics. Fourteenth-century natural philosophers accepted unconditionally the universal validity of the principle of causation: everything that exists and everything that occurs has a sufficient basis in reality, that is, has an efficient cause. It makes no difference what specific causes are involved in any particular case; they may be physical in nature or include acts of free will, the influence of heavenly forces, or the direct intervention of God. Scholastic thinkers did not require a closed physical context for causation; nothing like the law of conservation of energy existed to exclude the action of psychic or supernatural forces from playing a role in natural processes.[1] The only stipulation was that each of the causes in question, whether physical or psychic, terrestrial or celestial, natural or occult, had to have the characteristics of an efficient cause, that is, had to act like one.

Thus every event has an efficient cause, and, in particular, every motion has a motive cause. One of the most important fundamental principles of scholastic natural philosophy is that "everything that is moved is moved by something" *(omne quod movetur ab aliquo movetur)*. And when applied to inorganic processes, this principle takes the form that "everything that is moved is moved by *something else*"

---

1. Scholastic thinkers began to encounter difficulties only when they came to consider the idea of universal determinism. (Cf. *Die Vorläufer Galileis* [Rome: Edizioni di Storia e Letteratura, 1949], chap. 9.) If all processes in this world are determined by the motion of the heavens or, rather, by the action of the intelligences that move the heavens, and if God is the highest and ultimate cause standing behind the intelligences, then the question naturally arises, How is the free will of human beings to be reconciled with these deterministic assumptions? An act of will cannot be regarded as the effect of other causes; it cannot be an intermediate stage or the endpoint of a causal chain, but at most the beginning of one. Scholastic thinkers accepted this latter idea without hesitation, since the notion that free choices of the will can cause physical events does not conflict with any of the fundamental axioms of their metaphysics or physics.

(omne quod movetur ab alio movetur). Only living beings are really capable of moving themselves, since only they unite the mover (the soul) and the thing moved (the body) in the same subject. Otherwise, Aristotelian theory requires that the mover and the thing moved be different subjects. Scholastic thinkers accepted this assumption at first, but their ideas subsequently developed in another direction.

The active principle that makes a body a mover, that is, that enables it to move other objects, is called motive force *(vis motrix, vis motiva, virtus movens).* Conversely, a motive force is understood to be that which causes motion, and it is assumed that, all other things being equal, a constant force produces motion of constant velocity and that a changing force produces motion of changing velocity.

This idea represents the essential difference between scholastic and modern dynamics. There is, in addition, a basic disagreement regarding the nature of motion. For scholastic thinkers, motion is an intensible form, but in modern physics, it is change of position in absolute space and time. Together these differences make medieval mechanics look very unlike its modern counterpart. Modern physicists assume that a body in uniform motion [i.e., moving at a constant velocity in a straight line] needs no external force to maintain its state; it continues to move by itself. In this respect it is like a body at rest, which also maintains its state without the intervention of any external force. When a force does act on a body in uniform motion, it produces a change either in speed or direction. Scholastic thinkers, on the other hand, considered uniform motion to be the result of a constant motive force; in their view, no motion could occur unless some motive force was present, and every motion ceased as soon as the force causing it disappeared.

This topic will be discussed later in the chapter. First, however, it is necessary to ask what kinds of forces scholastic thinkers knew about and employed in constructing their theory of nature. In answering this question I will omit supernatural and occult forces and consider only terrestrial and natural ones. These fall into two classes: an agent operates either by nature *(a natura)* or by intellect *(ab intellectu).* The latter class includes forces that result from rational and willful choices, and if only the physical realm is considered, the class comprises the muscular force of animals and any other forces that derive either directly or indirectly from it. The former class, on the other hand, contains a group of inorganic, "natural" principles, the so-called elemental qualities, which are intrinsic properties of the four elements. All other qualities and inorganic forces are supposed to derive from them, although no real explanation of how this happens in specific cases was developed. The four elemental qualities are divided into two pairs of alterative qualities *(qualitates alterativae):* hot and cold, wet and dry. In addition, there exist two motive qualities *(qualitates motivae),* heaviness and lightness *(gravitas* and *levitas),* whose place in this scheme was, however, never entirely clear. Aristotle introduces them as secondary qualities, which means that they can be derived from the other qualities. But in another passage he treats them as primary, independent qualities. By and large scholastic thinkers adhered to the second interpretation and considered *gravitas* and *levitas* to be basic elemental qualities on the same level as the four primary qualities *(qualitates primae).*

These six, and they alone, were regarded as active qualities. The term *active* means that they, unlike other qualities, are able to act not only as formal causes, but also as efficient causes. For example, a hot object can make something else hot, and a cold object can make something else cold, but a white object cannot make another object white (at least not directly), and a hard object cannot make another object hard. In the case of *gravitas* and *levitas,* however, the situation is somewhat different, and this difference produced the doubts just mentioned about the true nature of these qualities. The problem is that a heavy object does not make something else heavy. The solution that finally found general acceptance regarded the motive qualities as being active in another sense, namely, insofar as they cause local motion.

Substantial forms, in contrast, are not active; that is, they cannot operate as active principles or function directly as efficient causes in natural processes.[2] The rule is that substantial forms can only act through their accidents, which means through their active qualities. Active qualities, on the other hand, can never func-

---

2. Only rarely did someone (such as William of Ockham) maintain that in special cases substantial forms can act directly.

tion as principal causes, but only as instrumental causes operating indirectly by virtue of the substantial form with which they are associated. Later critics of scholasticism considered causal explanations based on substantial forms to be particularly objectionable, but once the theory is correctly understood such explanations do not appear as misguided as they might at first glance. The situation is the same here as in the case of formal and final causes: when it came to giving an immediate, physical explanation of phenomena, the scholastics, like later scientists, demanded that the account be based on transitive causes or, in their terminology, on active principles. To search further for underlying final causes and substantial forms is the task of metaphysics and presents a different problem altogether.

What motive forces, strictly speaking, did scholastic thinkers recognize, that is, what forces did they think could function as direct causes of local motion? The answer is simple. I will omit for now natural motions, that is, gravitation and the upward motion of light substances, because they pose special problems; they will be considered further on. Otherwise, the only source of motion is animate muscle power and whatever other forces derive from it. Inorganic forces were generally not used to explain mechanical processes, although naturally it was understood that, for instance, local motion is produced when an object is heated or cooled. But scholastic thinkers did not consider hot and cold to be true motive forces, since they can only cause local motion indirectly, by means of the intermediate qualities of rarefaction and condensation *(raritas* and *densitas)* or in other similar ways.[3] Examples of real motive forces are the power of a horse pulling a wagon or the strength of Socrates (who always

3. Scholastic thinkers did not conceive of electrical forces, although they were familiar with some effects that in fact derive from them. Such occurrences were treated more or less as occult phenomena; in any case, no one sought a deeper explanation for them. And magnetic attraction, which was a well-known and much-discussed empirical fact, was not attributed to physical forces, but rather interpreted in a purely metaphysical fashion. An image *(species)* emanating from the magnet was thought to induce in the iron a striving for "perfection," that is, for union with the magnet, which is then transformed in some way into local motion without a real motive force being generated.

appears in such examples) carrying a stone. Such forces, which are organic in nature or depend on the exercise of the will, are in some ways problematical, since they involve a number of hard-to-define factors.

Forces of attraction and, generally, all forces that act at a distance are excluded on principle.[4] It is a fundamental axiom of scholastic-Aristotelian natural philosophy that action at a distance of whatever sort is barred from the realm of terrestrial forces. (Basically, this is also true in all later natural philosophy and natural science.) The only kind of causality admitted requires physical contact between the mover and the object moved.

This condition is fulfilled for the kinds of motion that scholastic thinkers considered normal, that is, motions resulting from the action of animate muscle power, as, for example, when an object is pushed, pulled, raised, or otherwise moved directly. In such cases the mover is different from the object moved, as the axiom "everything that is moved is moved by something else" requires, and the mover and its object are in contact.

There are, however, natural phenomena for which these two conditions are clearly not satisfied, either because no external mover is present or because the mover is not in contact with the object moved. The two classic examples are gravitational motion and projectile motion. A falling body moves even though no external mover, or at least no immediately perceptible one, is present. An arrow after it leaves the bow, or a stone after it leaves the thrower's hand, is no longer in contact with its mover. These two phenomena and the much-discussed problems they raised provided the stimulus to extend the principles of mechanics and to develop a unique

4. Here, too, there are exceptions. Occasionally someone (such as Roger Bacon and some of his followers) argued that gravitation actually involves attraction, and now and then the same was said of magnetism. The only philosopher, however, who consciously deviated from the predominant scholastic doctrine and accepted in a fundamental and general way the idea of forces acting at a distance was William of Ockham. (For Bacon see *An der Grenze von Scholastik und Naturphilosophie*, 2d ed. [Rome, Edizioni di Storia e Letteratura, 1952], p. 175 ff.; for Ockham see *Zwei Grundprobleme der scholastischen Naturphilosophie*, 2d ed. [Rome: Edizioni di Storia e Letteratura, 1951], p. 154 ff.)

concept of force. This concept, which is encountered neither in Aristotle nor in modern physics, is a product solely of late scholastic natural philosophy.

First let us consider the problem of gravitation.[5] The underlying foundation of the scholastic-Aristotelian theory of gravitation is the doctrine that every element has its natural place *(locus naturalis)*. Earth, the heaviest element, is the lowest or, more correctly, the innermost, since the center of the earth is the kernel around which all the other elements are arranged in concentric spheres according to their decreasing weights: water, then air, then fire. If a piece of an element is removed from its natural place, it attempts to return there. The motions that result from these attempts represent the natural motions of the elements. Thus, an element's striving to return to its natural place produces either gravity or levity. Strictly speaking, gravity pertains only to the pure element earth, and levity only to the pure element fire. The two intermediate elements, water and air (the two "media" of modern physics), can be relatively heavy or light depending on the place in which they happen to be. Compared to air and fire or, to use scholastic terminology, in the place of air or fire *(in loco aeris, ignis)*, water is heavy; compared to earth *(in loco terrae)*, it is light. A corresponding analysis applies to air.[6] But the "natural motions" of water and air were generally not a topic of interest. In their discussions of gravitation scholastic thinkers usually treated these two elements only as media and not as independent heavy or light objects. Finally, the gravity and levity of composite bodies *(corpora mixta)* is a separate problem that will be examined later.

The free fall of a body composed of the pure element earth represents the theoretical model for the study of the phenomenon of gravity.[7] Actually, scholastic theory does not allow the elements to occur in their pure forms, and references to purely heavy bodies are

5. For details of the scholastic theory of gravitation see *An der Grenze*, pp. 143–254.

6. In its true natural place an element is neither heavy nor light, since there no longer exists any tendency toward motion.

7. I will limit my discussion to this topic and not consider the upward motion of light bodies; scholastic philosophers usually did the same.

only abstractions that enable the concept of gravitation to be comprehended in an exact, theoretical fashion.

Scholastic thinkers were thus thoroughly acquainted with and occasionally used the methodological technique of abstraction, although in comparison with the modern approach they did not always make advantageous abstractions. Their theory of gravitation provides an example of this. In analyzing the problem of gravitational motion modern physics makes use of methodological simplifications, but they differ from those employed by scholastic thinkers. Motion is considered in a vacuum, that is, abstracted from the characteristics specific to the medium, but no limitations are placed on the nature of the object itself. The scholastic analysis takes the opposite approach: it presupposes the conceptually simplest kind of heavy body, but makes no provision for abstraction relative to the medium.[8] This standpoint derives from a number of fundamental assumptions that will be discussed further on.

It goes without saying that this formulation of the problem ensures that the scholastic treatment of gravitation will be entirely different from that developed by later physicists. One cannot say that scholastic thinkers set up the problem incorrectly, only that they did not set it up advantageously. They therefore not only had to make many detours to arrive at some correct results, but they also pursued many unnecessary and incorrect dead ends.

A heavy object outside its natural place attempts to return there. The natural place is correspondingly regarded as the final cause of the falling motion. We know, however, that this does not constitute a sufficient physical explanation. A final cause always presupposes a corresponding efficient cause. This, then, is the real problem, and it was considered to be one of the most difficult questions in phys-

---

8. For this reason, the assumption that the heavier a body is, the faster it falls, which is completely obvious in scholastic-Aristotelian philosophy and diametrically opposed to modern physical theory, is not entirely false. We think of free fall as happening in a vacuum, but scholastic philosophers imagined it taking place in a full medium *(medium plenum)*. Hence, from their point of view it is completely true that, for example, a piece of iron will fall faster than an equally large piece of a light and porous substance.

ics:[9] what is the active cause or, to phrase it differently, what is the motive force, the *movens,* that causes natural motion?

Aristotle considers gravitational motion to be a case of *motus ab alio,* motion that has an actual external mover. This mover has two aspects, one essential and the other accidental. The essential mover *(movens per se)* is the force that produced the heavy object, that is, the force that introduced the form of earth into the lump of primary matter or that made a quantum of earth out of a quantum of some other substance. Thus natural motion is caused by the generating agent *(a generante).* Scholastic-Aristotelian philosophy, however, regarded this generating agent *(generans)* as something extraterrestrial: the creation and dissolution of substances *(generatio* and *corruptio)* are caused by the intelligences that move the heavens. They are therefore also the essential and primary causes of gravitation.

In addition to the essential mover, however, there is also an accidental mover *(movens per accidens)* that actually produces the motion that occurs in each particular case. The *generans* cannot rightly be regarded as the mover of a heavy object that has already been created and is situated outside its natural place. Aristotle offers the following solution: the immediate mover is the *removens prohibens,* that is, the person (or thing) that removes the barrier to the fall, for example, the person who removes the surface on which the heavy object rests or who cuts the string from which it hangs. This is the accidental mover, since the change that it produces is not essential like the original creation of the heavy object.

It is not surprising that this solution was considered unsatisfactory. Averroes proposed another one that was, however, even less acceptable to scholastic thinkers. He theorized that the heavy object of its own accord sets the medium in motion and that the moving medium then pulls the object along with it, so that the object only moves itself in an accidental sense, just as a boatman who sets his boat in motion is afterward carried forward by it.

9. Nicoletto Vernias begins his *Quaestio* on the cause of gravitational motion (*Quaestio de gravibus et levibus* [Venice, 1504]) by remarking, "This question is the most difficult of all questions in physics."

The Averroistic theory only found a few adherents among scholastic philosophers.[10] On the whole, the scholastics preferred other approaches to solving the problem. In their view, the main question was this: The movers proposed by Aristotle suffice to set the heavy object in motion, but what moves the body that is already moving? Who continues the movement once it is initiated? For every motion there must be a mover. The answer that found fairly general acceptance was that the ultimate mover *(motor remotus)* is the *generans* and that the immediate mover *(motor proximus)* is the substantial form of the heavy object, which itself produces motion by means of the quality of gravity because substantial forms cannot act directly. In addition, the *removens prohibens* remains the accidental cause that initiates the motion.

The individual parts of this theory can be substantiated by reference to passages in Aristotle. Occasionally Aristotle says that the principle of gravitational motion is the nature *(natura)* of the heavy object; but something's nature can be understood to mean, among

10. In its genuine form it appears to have found no support whatsoever. Those philosophers who wanted to follow Averroes's theory of gravitation agreed with his contention that gravitational motion is not essential motion *(motus per se)*, but rather accidental motion *(motus per accidens)*. Averroes's notion of accidental was, however, completely reinterpreted in a variety of ways. Siger of Brabant provides an interesting example of this. In three different works he basically agrees with Averroes's theory by regarding natural motion as accidental. But in each of these works he interprets the meaning of "accidental" differently. The three works are the *Quaestiones naturales,* the *Impossibilia,* and the questions on Book II of the *Physics* discovered in Ms. Borgh. 114. (Cf. my article, "Nouvelles questions de Siger de Brabant sur la Physique d'Aristote," *Revue philosophique de Louvain* 44 (1946): 497 ff. [Now in *Ausgehendes Mittelalter,* vol. 2 (Rome: Edizioni di Storia e Letteratura, 1967), pp. 171–88.]). In the *Quaestiones in Physicam* attributed to Siger and edited in *Philosophes belges* XV, which are, however, of doubtful authenticity, the usual Aristotelian theory is advocated. (This caused me to think that Siger changed his mind about his theory of gravitation. See *An der Grenze,* pp. 159–60 and 225. Whether this really was the case or whether the questions do not in fact belong to him is not something I wish to decide.)

other things, its substantial form. And, as mentioned earlier, he also treated gravity and levity as qualities.

Within the framework of this theory of gravitation there occurred a remarkable change in the fourteenth century. The explanation itself remained the same, but the importance attributed to the individual elements shifted somewhat. There still remained the problem of specifying which of the three factors (the *generans*, the substantial form, and gravity) was, strictly speaking, the mover. Gradually, the accent shifted from the *generans*, which Aristotle took to be the real mover, first to the substantial form and then to gravity. In the process, the concept of motion caused by an external mover *(ab alio)* was gradually replaced by a concept of intrinsic motion *(ab intrinseco)*.

This shift in accent is not a mere nuance of interpretation, as may appear to be the case at first glance, but rather a fundamental transformation: the external mover, different from the object and in contact with it, is replaced as the principle of motion by a force that *inheres in* the moving object. Gravitational motion is therefore not caused by an external force, nor by the push or pull of an adjacent force—as the attempts at mechanistic explanations in the seventeenth century presupposed—nor by a force of attraction operating at a distance; it is instead a motion that carries its motive force within itself, in which the moving object strives as it were internally toward an external goal.[11] And the goal of this striving, but only the goal, is determined by the final cause, that is, by the natural place.

A similar development took place in the treatment of projectile motion. When a stone is thrown or an arrow is shot, what is the principle of motion once the projectile is separated from the original mover? Aristotle also considered this process to be motion caused by an external mover *(motus ab alio)* and theorized that the

11. This idea is still inferior to the famous interpretation given by Copernicus (*De revolutionibus orbium caelestium*, cap. 9; cf. *An der Grenze*, pp. 173–74). Copernicus's interpretation is generally regarded as the first formulation of the law of gravitational attraction of masses, but such an approach is much too modern.

original mover imparts to the medium a secondary force which then moves the projectile forward while becoming progressively weaker, until it finally dies out. In the fourteenth century this idea was replaced by the so-called theory of impetus, which asserts that the original mover imparts a secondary force, called impetus, not to the air but to the projectile itself, and that this impetus, acting as an inherent force, moves the projectile onward after its separation from the original mover. This motion likewise results from the striving of an internal force toward a goal; again, the direction of this striving, and only the direction, is determined by a final cause. This time, however, the final cause is not established by nature *(a natura)* as in gravitation, but rather by intellect *(ab intellectu)*; the motion is determined by the thrower's goal. But, as always, the cause that really produces the motion is the corresponding efficient cause, in this case the impetus.

Some people have wanted to regard this theory of impetus as a precursor of the law of inertia,[12] but this is out of the question. The concept of an inherent force that moves the object it belongs to is, in fact, the exact opposite of the law of inertia. It is an idea that derives from the axiom *omne quod movetur ab aliquo movetur:* every motion needs a mover, not only to initiate it, but also to maintain it. In those cases in which no external mover is present, an inherent force is a sufficient substitute; this is the improvement on Aristotle's conception that scholastic thinkers introduced. The law of inertia of modern mechanics, of course, says the opposite: a uniform motion continues by itself without needing any force for its maintenance. That is a fundamentally different idea that cannot be considered analogous to the theory of impetus.

To summarize, scholastic mechanics recognized two kinds of motive force in the strict sense. The first group includes those forces that produce motion from the outside *(ab alio)*, that is, in which the mover and the thing moved are different objects but in contact. The second group includes those forces that operate from the inside *(ab intrinseco)*, that is, in which the motive force inheres in the moving

12. Cf. *Die Vorläufer Galileis*, chap. 6 [and the essays translated in chaps. 4 and 5 below].

object, or, in other words, in which the force moves its own subject rather than some other one. There are two types of inherent force: one occurs in the form of gravity and levity as the motive principle of natural motion; the other in the form of impetus as the cause of violent motion in projectiles.

The first kind of force is, of course, encountered not only in scholastic-Aristotelian natural philosophy, but in modern mechanics as well. At most there exists a difference in approach. Modern thinkers consider mechanical forces exclusively in the abstract and are only interested in their magnitude, while scholastic natural philosophers admitted the whole range of objective factors, in all their concreteness, into their physical deliberations. When, for instance, they reckoned the force with which Socrates lifts or moves a stone, they also took into account secondary, contingent factors that depend on organic or volitional considerations. In the later fourteenth century an increasing level of abstraction gradually becomes perceptible: the forces were represented by letters, as they are today, and only in special cases did the question of constraints involving concrete secondary conditions arise. Above all, scholastic thinkers began to distinguish between physically essential and unessential secondary conditions and to take only the former into account. Thus, in this regard no difference exists in principle between late scholastic and modern mechanics.

But the situation is different in the case of the second group of motive forces; neither Aristotelian nor modern physics recognizes inherent motive forces. This is an entirely novel idea that gave fourteenth-century dynamics its highly original character, and it constitutes one of the most important and most characteristic features of the late medieval view of nature.

II

The dynamics of motion, however, cannot be explained by reference to motive forces alone. In peripatetic physics not only a motive force, but also a resistive force *(vis resistiva)* is needed if motion is to occur, since the function of resistance is to generate the element of succession in motion. Scholastic natural philosophy assumes that in theory every cause acts instantaneously;[13] thus if no other factor were to interfere, a motive force would produce its effect instantaneously *(in instanti),* not successively and in time *(in tempore).* There would be no motion, only mutation. The factor that makes changes happen successively is resistance; consequently, scholastic thinkers regarded resistance simply as the "cause of succession in motion" *(causa successionis in motu).* The greater the resistance is in relation to the motive force, the stronger, naturally, is its impeding and retarding effect. If the motive and resistive forces are equal, they will balance each another, and no motion will occur.[14] If, however, the motive force is greater than the resistance, the velocity of the resulting motion will vary according to how much greater the force is than the resistance. In other words, the velocity depends on the ratio of motive force to resistance. The specific relationship involved will be considered later [see chap. 3], but it should be mentioned here that it is not one of simple proportionality, at least not for fourteenth-century thinkers.

The next question is, What different kinds of resistance did scholastic physics recognize? If one disregards alterative forces *(vires alterativae)*—for instance, when a body is heated, its coldness acts as

13. Occasionally one encounters the idea (derived from Alhazen) that effects are not actually produced instantaneously but rather with infinite velocity. We read, for instance, in Peter John Olivi *(Sent.* II, qu. 26; in Jansen's ed., vol. 2, p. 448): "It is the opinion of some students of perspective, such as the author of the *Perspectiva* (i.e., Alhazen), that corporeal agents cause their impressions in time, although this is imperceptible to us." As the fourteenth century progresses, this opinion appears more frequently, especially in regard to the propagation of light, which is not thought to happen in a durationless instant but rather in an infinitely small period of time. This theory gradually finds general acceptance. On the other hand, the idea that light itself has a finite velocity is never mentioned.

14. This is also true if the resistance is greater than the motive force, at least if the former is not itself an active force, as, for example, when Socrates tries to move a stone whose resistance exceeds his powers. In those cases in which two active forces operate on each other, it is tacitly assumed that the larger is the motive force and the smaller the resistive force.

a resistance, and the change in temperature takes place more slowly when this resistance is greater—and limits the discussion to true mechanical resistances, then the answer is as follows. On the one hand, there are contrary forces, that is, violent forces that act on (or in) the moving object and contrary to the motive force (or at least have components contrary to the motive force). These would include any external push or pull applied to a moving object as well as an impetus imparted to it. On the other hand, there exist certain internal tendencies of the moving object, and they are particularly interesting since they reveal once more, but from a different perspective, the characteristic features that make late medieval dynamics fundamentally different from modern physics. The first of these internal tendencies that manifest themselves as resistance is the striving of every material substance to reach its natural place and to remain there once it has attained this goal. This is the source of gravity and levity, which were mentioned earlier in the chapter as motive forces. When Socrates tries to lift a stone, he encounters a resistance that he perceives as weight[15] and that is nothing more than the striving of the stone to remain in its natural place.

The second internal tendency is the striving of every body already situated in its natural place to remain at rest or, if set in motion, to return to a state of rest. This form of resistance comes into play when an object moves horizontally, whereas the first type only opposes vertical movements. For instance, a horse pulling a wagon only experiences the second kind of resistance, since the wagon is located in its natural place and the force of gravity is therefore not a factor. But the impetus that moves an arrow or stone in flight is opposed not only by gravity, but also by the striving of the object to return to a state of rest. Thus scholastic thinkers had a good understanding, at least in principle, of how to analyze a motion or the motive force producing it into component parts, even without using a force parallelogram.

15. Weight *(pondus)* and gravity *(gravitas)* are considered to be identical: weight is nothing more than the hindrance of a tendency toward motion. In this regard the scholastics saw things more clearly than many seventeenth-century natural philosophers.

This striving to remain at rest or to return to a state of rest can be called the *inertia* of material substances, but it must be noted that only half of this scholastic "law of inertia" agrees with the modern law. In both medieval and modern mechanics a body at rest attempts to remain in a state of rest. But in modern theory a body in a state of uniform motion has the tendency to persist in that motion, while scholastic philosophers thought it would tend to return to a state of rest. The difference between these two concepts is of fundamental importance.[16] Corresponding to these two different ideas of inertia there are two different definitions of the concept of force. In scholastic theory a motive force causes motion of constant velocity, while in modern theory it causes changes in velocity, that is, acceleration.

In addition to these first two "natural tendencies"—gravity (or levity) and inertia—there is also a third that operates somewhat differently. Every material substance strives for "continuity,"[17] which means that it resists any attempt to tear it apart. This tendency manifests itself not only when, for instance, an axe splits a piece of wood, but also in the resistance that the medium offers to a moving object and hence indirectly to the mover. This latter phenomenon (which is of course more important to the general theory of mechanics) is what in modern terminology is called friction.[18]

16. Cf. *Die Vorläufer Galileis,* chap. 6 [and the essay translated in chap. 4 below].

17. "Each natural body seeks its own continuity, because a unified force is stronger than one divided" (Buridan, *Physica* IV, qu. 9). It appears that Roger Bacon first introduced this concept.

18. Unlike modern mechanics, however, scholastic philosophy makes no fundamental distinction between these three kinds of resistance. Modern physical theory regards a body's weight and the friction of the medium as true mechanical forces that are just like motive forces and can therefore be subtracted from them (or resolved using a force parallelogram when this applies). The inertial resistance of masses, on the other hand, is a different kind of factor that involves division. Only this latter factor, moreover, plays a role in the interrelation of force, matter, and acceleration. (The force is proportional to the product of mass and acceleration,

Usually all three types of resistance operate together,[19] but there are also cases in which one or another of the components disappears. An example of this has already been given: a horse pulling a wagon must overcome only the inertia of the load and the friction of the medium. (The friction of the surface on which he moves is not taken into account.) When, on the other hand, a stone is thrown straight up in the air, only gravity and the resistance of the medium oppose the impetus that moves it. A body in free fall likewise encounters no resistance due to inertia, and therefore only the friction of the medium impedes its motion—at least this is so if only purely heavy bodies are considered. We know, however, that the concept of a pure element was an abstraction for scholastic thinkers. In reality they considered all material substances to be so-called *mixta*, composites of all four elements combined in various proportions. Heavy objects that actually occur in nature are therefore only compounds in which the heavy components predominate, but which also contain light elements. The levity of these light elements, however, also produces a resistance that must be taken into account in the case of free fall.

---

or, in other words, acceleration is a function of the quotient of force divided by inertial resistance.) Fourteenth-century thinkers, however, immediately assumed that *all* resistances are similar in nature both to each other and to all motive forces. (In modern terminology, all of them would have the same physical "dimension.") As a result, the basic rule that velocity is determined by the proportion of force to resistance was extended to include all types of resistance. This too is one of the essential differences between the physical concepts of the fourteenth century and those of the modern age.

19. Thomas Aquinas (*Physica* IV, lect. 12) formulates the usual theory as follows: "This resistance can be of three types. The first results from the position of the object, for the mover attempts to transfer the object to one place, while the object itself, being in another place, resists the attempt of the mover. The second results from the nature of the object, as becomes clear in violent motions, such as when a heavy object is thrown upwards. The third results from the medium. All three should be considered together as one resistance so that one cause of slowness in motion is produced."

This distinctive theory, which only reached its full development in the fourteenth century, is of interest because it illuminates certain difficulties in scholastic mechanics that derived from the subject's basic concepts. The source of these difficulties was the problem of free fall in a vacuum. Since the only form of resistance opposing gravity during free fall is the friction of the medium, it follows that free fall in a vacuum (if one could exist) would take place without resistance and hence instantaneously. Aristotle accepted this conclusion without further consideration and used it as one of his proofs against the existence of a vacuum. But scholastic thinkers were also aware of another theory, which had been proposed by Avempace, and they preferred it to Aristotle's. Avempace's writings have not survived and were already lost in the scholastic period, but his theory concerning free fall in a vacuum was summarized in detail by Averroes, although only in order to refute it. Avempace argued that natural motion in a vacuum would not take place instantaenously, but rather at a certain normal velocity, and that the friction of the medium merely modifies this velocity. This idea is, in fact, correct and has been incorporated into modern physical theory. And it was this idea that scholastic thinkers tried to prove using the assumptions of Aristotelian natural philosophy.

The attempt was made in two phases. In the first phase, which had already begun under Albertus Magnus and Thomas Aquinas, it was proved that a body can only traverse an extended continuum in successive stages, regardless of circumstances. This successiveness was immediately interpreted to mean that the motion must take place with a certain finite velocity. Not until the fourteenth century did someone arrive at the insight—Nicole Oresme was apparently the first person to state it—that the proof that such motions take place successively says nothing about their velocity and that, on the contrary, the motion would occur infinitely quickly. The proposed solution, Oresme concludes, represents no advance over Aristotle's theory of instantaneous motion, since his instant in the sense of a measureless moment is replaced by an instant in the sense of an infinitely small space of time. Thus an attempt was made to solve the problem from another angle by attributing to composite bodies an inner resistance that in a heavy object results from the levity of its light components and, conversely, in a light object results from the gravity of its heavy components. The total gravity of all the heavy parts is compared to the total levity of all the light ones; the greater of the two factors is considered to be the motive force and the lesser, the resistive force. The conclusion is that the velocity of free fall is determined by the ratio of the two forces.[20] Needless to say, the actual calculation of these factors was never contemplated. Only the basic problem itself was addressed, and it was solved by discovering a resistance that does not disappear in a vacuum and that therefore allows Avempace's theory to be explained using Aristotelian principles.[21]

All the difficulties caused for scholastic thinkers by the problem of free fall derived from their theory of the natural dispositions of material bodies. No such things exist in modern mechanics. According to the modern law of inertia, a body has no tendency to motion whatsoever, but simply strives to maintain its state, be it one of rest or of uniform motion. This applies to gravity as well. In modern theory gravity is not an internal principle of motion, but rather an external force that, like any other, must overcome the inertial resistance of the object to be moved. And this resistance, of course, remains even in a vacuum. Only the relatively

20. From this it follows that all compound bodies with identical compositions *(mixta eiusdem compositionis)* will fall at the same speed in a vacuum regardless of their weights. For scholastic philosophers, however, this result represented an objection against the proposed theory rather than an argument in its favor.

21. Another law of nature inherited from antiquity was also explained theoretically on the basis of these same principles. This was Archimedes's law and its corollaries, which postulate the dependence of a body's weight on the nature of the medium [surrounding it] or, in Aristotelian terminology, on the nature of the place in which it is located. Water is relatively heavy and air relatively light, while an element in its true natural place is neither heavy nor light. I have discussed this problem in detail in *An der Grenze*, p. 236 ff. and therefore will not deal with it again here. . . .

small friction of the medium disappears. Thus free fall in a vacuum, which constituted a difficult problem for scholastic natural philosophy, represents the pure, unhindered form of falling motion in modern mechanics.[22]

22. Gravitational motion also represented a serious problem for scholastic dynamics in another respect, but in this case natural philosophers were successful in devising a solution. According to scholastic theory, a constant force gives rise to a constant velocity as long as the resistance remains unchanged. Thus accelerated motion presupposes either an increasing force or a decreasing resistance. If some animate force or an impetus causes the motion, then this condition can immediately be regarded as satisfied. In gravitational motion, however, the situation is different. Gravity is unquestionably a constant force (a body's weight, of course, does not change because it moves), yet gravitational motion is not uniform but accelerated. Naturally, this fact was known empirically not only in the Middle Ages but also in antiquity. This is yet another problem that does not exist in modern mechanics. In modern theory, a constant force by its very nature always produces uniformly accelerated motion. The scholastic concept of force, on the other hand, made the problem anything but easy, and solutions of every possible variety were proposed. (For details see *An der Grenze*, p. 181 ff.) The most interesting and ingenious of these is that conceived by Buridan and his school. The acceleration of gravitational motion is explained with the aid of the theory of impetus. Gravity produces in the heavy object not only a (constant) motion, but also an impetus, and this "acquired impetus" adds to the gravity and strengthens it. The process repeats itself anew at every instant (in contrast to projectile motion, where the process occurs only once), since gravity continues to operate, and the result is that [the motive force] and hence the speed of descent continually increase. This is a thoroughly plausible explanation of the acceleration of gravitational motion, and one encounters its main features again in the seventeenth century, advocated by no less a thinker than Huygens. Moreover, it shows once again that empirical data can be interpreted on the basis of fundamentally different assumptions in such a way that the results are "correct" from both perspectives.

Three:

THE CONCEPT OF
THE FUNCTION IN
FOURTEENTH-CENTURY PHYSICS

For Anneliese Maier, what most distinguishes fourteenth-century natural philosophers is their new sense of independence vis-à-vis Aristotle's explanations of natural phenomena and their confidence in their own ability to find better explanations using the tools of logic. Although they stopped short of rejecting the fundamental axioms of Aristotelian cosmology, they did improve on Aristotle's theories in numerous contexts, especially in the field of mechanics. As mentioned in chapter 2, they held firm to the axiom that "everything that is moved is moved by something," but reinterpreted the application of this principle to free fall and projectile motion and in the process developed the uniquely scholastic concept of inherent force. This next selection likewise focuses on the concepts of motive force and resistance, but here the question is not "What forces are involved in motion?" but rather "How are the velocities of moving objects related to the forces producing them?" Aristotle never fully answered this latter question, and not until the fourteenth century was a more comprehensive theory developed.

The breakthrough was achieved by Thomas Bradwardine (d. 1349) in his Tractatus de Proportionibus, *published in 1328. Bradwardine was a logician, philosopher, and theologian at Merton College, Oxford, the first of several distinguished mathematicians and natural philosophers at the college.*

His most illustrious successors at Merton were William Heytesbury, Richard Swineshead, and John Dumbleton, all of whom made important contributions to the mathematical description of motion. Maier refers to these four men and their characteristic mathematical approach to problems of natural philosophy as the "Oxford school" to distinguish them from the Parisian school of Jean Buridan and his successors. Bradwardine himself left Oxford sometime after 1335 and in 1349 became Archbishop of Canterbury, only to die in the same year of the plague.

The essay translated here likewise represents a breakthrough, in this case in the study of medieval science. The field was virtually invented by Pierre Duhem, but his researches centered on Buridan and the Parisian school and he patriotically regarded the University of Paris as the only creative force in fourteenth-century natural philosophy. In his view, Bradwardine and the other Mertonians were tolerable mathematicians but uninventive scientists. Today this bias has been swept away, and the Oxford school has become one of the main objects of current research. Part of the credit for initiating this change must go to Anneliese Maier. In her groundbreaking essay, "Der Funktionsbegriff in der Physik des 14. Jahrhunderts" (Divus Thomas 24 [1946]: 147–66), *she pointed out the correct interpretation of a key element of Bradwardine's proportional mathematics and showed that, in light of this interpretation, his* Tractatus *must be regarded as one of the major monuments of fourteenth-century natural philosophy.*

Maier's original insight into the importance of the Tractatus de Proportionibus *for the history of medieval science is now generally acknowledged. The standard edition of and introduction to the* Tractatus is Thomas of Bradwardine, His Tractatus de Proportionibus, *edited and translated by H. Lamar Crosby, Jr. (Madison, Wis.: University of Wisconsin Press, 1955). A short but very useful discussion of Bradwardine's law and the mathematics of proportions can be found in John Murdoch and Edith Sylla, "The Science of Motion," in* Science in the Middle Ages, *edited by David Lindberg (Chicago: University of Chicago Press, 1978), pp. 224–26 and 230–31. A good introduction to the Mertonians in general is given in chapter 4, "The Emergence of Kinematics at Merton College," in Marshall Clagett,* The Science of Mechanics in the Middle Ages *(Madison, Wis.: University of Wisconsin Press, 1959).*

The translation that follows is an excerpt from "Der Funktionsbegriff in der Physik des 14. Jahrhunderts" as published in Die Vorläufer Galileis

(Rome: Edizioni di Storia e Letteratura, 1949), but taking into account Maier's revisions appended to the second edition (Rome: Edizioni di Storia e Letteratura, 1966), pp. 325-26. The selection covers pages 81-93 of the original text. I have omitted Maier's discussion of Bradwardine's influence on later thinkers. Supplementary reading on this topic in English can be found in the works mentioned above. In a few cases in which Crosby's edition of the Tractatus *is superior to the Latin text that Maier used, I have tacitly substituted the former for the latter.* Velocitas *is translated as "velocity" rather than "speed" on the assumption that no one will read back the modern vector concept into the medieval term.* Potentia *is translated as "force" rather than "power," since most modern discussions refer to the ratio of motive power to resistive power simply (if inaccurately) as the ratio of force to resistance.*

The most important methodological tool of modern physics, the technique that by itself made exact natural science possible, is the use of mathematical functions in the description of natural processes. It is therefore understandable that ever since Duhem's researches drew attention to fourteenth-century physics, and some thinkers began to credit this body of knowledge with preparing the way for or even anticipating classical mechanics, it has often been asked whether and to what extent late scholastic philosophers worked with functions.

In the ensuing discussion of this question it was frequently overlooked that the answer depends first and foremost upon what the term *function* is understood to mean. The concept of function can be interpreted in various ways, and its definition has changed several times since its formal introduction into mathematics. It is obvious that late scholastic philosophers did not think of functions in the same way as modern mathematicians do; it is, however, equally obvious that not only the scholastics but Aristotle as well were well acquainted with the phenomenon of functional dependence. Otherwise, a science of motion in the most general sense would not have been possible. They knew, of course, that dependency relationships exist in nature in the sense that a change in one variable is contingent upon a change in another. A larger force, for instance, produces a greater effect, the distance traversed in local motion increases with time, and a body's weight depends on its size, all other things being equal. Moreover, they understood that in many cases these dependency relationships demonstrate a certain regularity. But the question is, Did they attempt to comprehend *this regularity itself,* and, if so, to what extent were they successful? For regardless of how it is defined in detail, the mathematical function still has one essential characteristic: it is a computational formula that expresses the dependency relationship between two (or more) variables.[1]

In modern practice a function can be represented in two ways: with an equation using mathematical symbols or with a curve in a coordinate system. Both of these possibilities were unknown in the fourteenth century. Strictly speaking, for an equation to be a function it must contain variable quantities, whereas a normal algebraic equation only expresses the relationship between fixed (known or unknown) quantities. This use of equations to represent functions only appeared toward the end of the seventeenth century; even Galileo was unfamiliar with it. A similar observation applies to the representation of functions in a coordinate system. Various writers, following Duhem, have wanted to regard the development of graphical symbols by Nicole Oresme[2] as the very beginning of analytic geometry, but they are mistaken. Certainly Oresme's method of graphical representation presupposes an understanding of functional dependence; the idea can be found in a variety of his works and was by no means unusual by the middle of the fourteenth century. But Oresme's method is not intended to emphasize depen-

1. A classic case of the attempt to formulate a dependency relationship using a mathematical function is the famous dispute over the measurement of forces that took place in the seventeenth century. It was clear to everyone that a moving body's capacity to produce an effect (for instance, the effect of an arrow or other projectile) depends on its velocity. This was already known in antiquity and the Middle Ages. The question on which the controversy centered concerned the exact nature of this dependency. Is the "living force" simply proportional to the velocity, as Descartes and his school maintained, or is it a function of the square of the velocity, as Leibniz argued?

2. Cf. *Die Vorläufer Galileis* (Rome: Edizioni di Storia e Letteratura, 1949), chap. 5.

dency relationships per se, which is the crucial point. His purpose in using geometric techniques was entirely different.

Therefore, if late scholastic thinkers were actually acquainted with functions and used them in their physics, the functions must have been formulated in some other fashion. The only mode of expression available at that time was what historians of mathematics have labeled *verbal algebra:* a literal calculus that used letters to stand for the quantities involved in the calculations, but that did not employ symbols to represent the relationships between the quantities or the operations to be performed on them. The relationships and operations were described in words.[3] If, for example, Socrates was assumed to be moving twice as fast as Plato, the two velocities were not represented as a and $a/2$; instead, one velocity was labeled a and the other b, and the statement was added that b is half of a. Another serious deficiency was the lack of an equals sign or a substitute for it, which meant that relationships of equality always had to be specified in words.

Nevertheless, these are all formal, external considerations that only concern the communication of what is known and not the knowledge itself. Scholastic thinkers were actually well acquainted with mathematical equations, only instead of expressing them with simple and clearly arranged formulas, they used a heavy and often obscure language. It must be expected, therefore, that these same limitations will apply to their formulation of functions—if they indeed understood the concept.

With these considerations in mind, we can now ask whether scholastic thinkers in fact employed functions (expressed in terms of the available formal structure) to describe and explain natural processes. Did they attempt to discover exact computational formulas of this sort; did they even recognize the problem that is involved here? And if the answer is yes, did their efforts lead to results; did they in this regard advance beyond Aristotle and high scholasticism?

3. This is the same literal calculus that invaded virtually every field of knowledge in the early fourteenth century, even those unsuited to quantitative analysis. It is the mode of expression employed in the notorious technique of "calculations." (Cf. *Die Vorläufer Galileis,* pp. 97–98 and 113–114.)

I believe that these questions must be answered in the affirmative. And if trivial forms of dependency are ignored (for example, at a constant velocity twice the distance is covered in twice the time, and a piece of steel is half as heavy as another twice its size), there is one particular branch of physics in which these developments were accomplished, namely, dynamics.

In scholastic-Aristotelian philosophy, every motion arises from the action of a motive force against a resistance.[4] There is no motion without a motive force ("everything that is moved is moved by something"), nor is there motion without resistance. A force that is not opposed by some resistance will act instantaneously, and the resulting change of position will take place in one jump, not in successive stages. Finally, motion only occurs when the force is able to overcome the resistance, that is, when the *vis motiva* is greater than the *vis resistiva*. If the motive force is equal to or smaller than the resistance, it is unable to act and no motion occurs. If it is stronger than the resistance, the velocity of the resulting motion will be directly proportional to the magnitude of the force and inversely proportional to the magnitude of the resistance. In other words, the velocity is determined by the relationship between the force and the resistance.[5]

This principle is the basis of all Aristotelian dynamics. Aristotle states it repeatedly in different forms according to the context in which he is using it, and for him it constitutes the self-evident precondition for any discussion of motion. Moreover, in the seventh book of the *Physics*[6] he presents a number of specific rules that are meant to illustrate this fundamental principle of dynamics, al-

4. This applies to all types of motion, but in reality even Aristotle considers only local motion in detail. He contents himself with a brief application of the results to the cases of alteration and augmentation, and scholastic thinkers followed him in this regard, at least at first.

5. Buridan, *Physica* I, qu. 12: "No effect is produced from a proportion of equality or lesser inequality between the agent and the resistance. It is necessary for the active force to excede the resistive force, and the larger the proportion of greater inequality is between the agent and the resistance, the greater will be the strength of the agent, or the velocity it produces, or the distance through which it acts."

6. Aristotle, *Physica* VII, cap. 5.

though he does not summarize them in a general formula. The search for such a formula was the problem whose solution led to the development of functional equations in the fourteenth century.

The Aristotelian rules are as follows. If mover A moves an object B in the time period D through a distance C, then the same force or an equivalent one will move half of B in the time period D through twice the distance C, or it will move half of B in half of D through the whole distance C. Averroes provides a simplified version of these two rules: the same force A will move half of B with twice the velocity. Furthermore, the same force A will move the object B in half the time through half the distance, or half the force will move half the object through the entire distance in the full time period. The converse, on the other hand, which states that half the force will move the whole object at half the velocity or that the full force will move twice the object at half the velocity, does not hold. It can happen that under these conditions no motion will occur at all, if halving the force (or doubling the object) makes the force equal to or less than the resistance. Finally, twice the force will move twice the object with the same velocity with which the original force moved the original object.

What these rules essentially say is that doubling the motive force or halving the resistance results in twice the velocity, all other things being equal. But is is not always the case that halving the force or doubling the resistance will result in half the velocity. Motion only occurs if the force continues to be greater than the resistance after the changes have been made.

The commentaries on Aristotle's *Physics* written in the thirteenth century and the first three decades of the fourteenth century avoid discussing this chapter entirely or are content to provide a simple recapitulation and explanation of Aristotle's meaning without raising any new questions.[7] No generalization of the rules is attempted,

7. One finds a surprising deviation in Albertus Magnus, *Physica* VII, tract. II, cap. 5 (Borgnet's ed.): "If quantity A moves quantity B through the whole length C in the whole time D . . . then a similar quantity will move half of B in the same time D through a space *a little larger (paulo longius)* than C." But a comparison with the older printings, such as those of Venice, 1494 and 1517, shows that the editor made an error here. The text must read "twice as long" *(duplo longius)* as C."

and the cases that are considered are limited to Aristotle's examples of doubling and halving each of the factors. At most, the commentators try to formulate the rules somewhat more simply and arrange them more clearly.[8]

Thomas Bradwardine was the first thinker to approach the problem in a general fashion. In his *Tractatus proportionum,* written in 1328, he attempts to find the precise mathematical rule that defines the interdependence of force, resistance, and velocity.[9] The physical aspect of the problem is regarded as established fact. His only objective is to formulate the physical relationships mathematically. Thus, it is completely justified to say that it is simply a matter of finding a functional equation that adequately represents the fundamental principles of dynamics.[10] The desired function has to satisfy the following conditions: if the force and resistance form a "proportion of greater inequality" (that is, if the motive force is greater than the resistance), then the velocity depends upon the quotient[11] of the two quantities; if, however, they form a "proportion of equality or of

8. They also try to formulate the concepts of force and resistance more precisely than Aristotle did and attempt, in particular, to take into account a number of secondary conditions that could modify the effect. These efforts gradually led the commentators to replace the absolute values of force and resistance in their calculations with the "capacity to act" *(posse agere)* and the "capacity to resist" *(posse resistere).* But the accepted principles of dynamics remained unchanged by these modifications.

9. I used the edition printed in Venice, 1505, with occasional corrections from the manuscripts Vat. lat. 1108, fol. 69–81; ibid., fol. 104–119v; Vat. lat. 2185, fol. 23v–27v; Vat. lat. 4429, fol. 23–29; and Ottob. lat. 179, fol. 92–98. [Additional comments from the second edition of *Die Vorläufer Galileis,* p. 325.] Bradwardine's *Tractatus* is now available in a modern edition that, although not really a critical edition, is based on a sufficiently large number of manuscripts: H. L. Crosby, Jr., *Thomas of Bradwardine, His Tractatus de proportionibus* (Madison, Wis.: University of Wisconsin Press, 1955). Cf. also my review of this book in *Isis* 48 (1957): 84 ff.

10. One could almost say that Bradwardine wanted to write the *Principia mathematica philosophiae naturalis* of his century.

11. "Proportion" in scholastic terminology always means quotient (or fraction) and does not involve any comparative element.

lesser inequality" (that is, if the force is less than or equal to the resistance), then the velocity must be zero.

Bradwardine's *Tractatus* begins[12] with these words:

> It happens[13] that every successive motion is proportional to another in velocity. Hence natural philosophy, which considers motion, ought not to ignore the proportion of motions and of velocities in motions. And because this knowledge is necessary and very difficult, and has not been fully treated in any branch of philosophy, we have written this work on the proportion of the velocities of motions.

The topic of discussion is thus not velocities as such and how they depend on motive force and resistance, but rather the "proportions of velocities in motions," that is, differences and changes in velocities. How is a change in velocity contingent on a change in force or resistance? This is the subject of the treatise. And the changes that are considered include not only halving and doubling, as in Aristotle, but also any arbitrary ratio of the variables to one another.

The treatise is divided into four chapters, the first of which furnishes the necessary mathematical background for calculating with proportions. The second contains an enumeration and refutation "in the fashion of Aristotle" of various erroneous viewpoints. The third chapter presents Bradwardine's own correct theory, and the fourth discusses several rather unusual technical problems.[14]

Bradwardine opens the second chapter with the statement that "there are four incorrect opinions regarding the subject under consideration." They are as follows. "First, it is maintained that the proportion of velocities in motions follows the excess of the force

12. The prologue that precedes the *Tractatus* in the printed edition is not by Bradwardine.

13. The printed edition reads *convenit,* while the manuscript tradition clearly reads *contingit.* We thank Msgr. Pelzer for pointing this out.

14. It treats the problem of rotational motion but from a kinematic rather than a dynamic viewpoint. Bradwardine asks, What is the velocity of a body whose individual parts move at different speeds? This was a much discussed question, and Bradwardine was by no means the first one to raise it, although it usually came up in another context. (Cf. *Die Vorläufer Galileis,* chap. 5.)

of the mover over the force of the thing moved," that is, that the ratio of the velocities depends upon the [ratio of the differences] between the force and resistance.[15] This theory . . . is immediately rejected. It was sometimes attributed to Averroes, who remarks in his commentary on Aristotle's rules that "it is so that the velocity appropriate to any motion follows the 'excess' of the motive force over the force of the thing moved."[16]

The second incorrect theory asserts that "the proportion [of velocities] in motions follows the proportion of the excess of [the force of] the mover over the force of the thing moved," that is, that the ratio of the velocities is determined by the ratio of [the quotients obtained by dividing the difference between the force and the resistance by the resistance].[17] This theory is also immediately rejected, as is the fourth and last one, which states that "there is no proportion nor any excess of motive force over resistive force." What is meant here is that magnitudes of intensity such as force and resistance are not measurable and are therefore not capable of quantitative comparison. From the standpoint of scholastic philosophy, of course, this is theoretically a valid objection. Bradwardine disposes of it by citing numerous passages in Aristotle and Averroes in which magnitudes of intensity are regarded as real quantities and proportions between them are permitted. He also gives an example from experience, namely, music.

The only theory that Bradwardine really takes into consideration and refutes in earnest is the third one, which asserts that "the proportion of velocities in motions follows the proportion of the [resistances of the] objects given the same or an equivalent mover, and follows the proportion of the movers given the same or an equivalent object."[18] Although this theory appears to be supported

15. If V_1 and V_2 are the velocities, F_1 and F_2 the motive forces, and R_1 and R_2 the resistances, then according to this theory the following equation would be valid: $V_1 : V_2 = (F_1 - R_1) : (F_2 - R_2)$.

16. Averroes, *Physica* VII, comm. 35 (Venice, 1550).

17. $V_1 : V_2 = \dfrac{(F_1 - R_1)}{R_1} : \dfrac{(F_2 - R_2)}{R_2}$

18. This solution could be written in symbols as $V = F : R$.

by a number of passages in Aristotle and Averroes and is capable of rational demonstration, Bradwardine argues that it is wrong in two respects: "this position can be refuted in two ways, first on account of insufficiency, and second on account of incorrectness." It is insufficient because it does not take into account those cases in which both the mover and the object moved change; and it is incorrect because it entails that "any object can be moved by any mover." If a given force moves an object at a certain velocity, then according to this rule it will move twice the object at half the velocity, four times the object at a quarter of the velocity, and so on to infinity. In other words, this solution does not allow for the fact that the force must always be greater than the resistance, and that if the opposite is true or the two are equal, then no motion whatsoever will result. But this means that one of the essential conditions that the desired rule must satisfy is not fulfilled.

Bradwardine presents these rejected theories (except the fourth, which has a different character from the others) in a form that makes them nothing other than so many functional equations expressed in the only idiom available to scholastic thinkers. They are computational formulas stated in the unwieldy language of the fourteenth century that can, however, be easily translated into modern mathematical symbols and that express the relationship between specific values of one dependent variable (velocity) and two independent variables (force and resistance). But they are incorrect solutions because they either do not account for the stipulated physical conditions or only do so inadequately.

"Since, therefore, the clouds of ignorance have been driven away by the winds of demonstration, all that remains is for truth to shine forth with the light of knowledge." These words introduce the third chapter, in which Bradwardine finally presents the "correct" solution. "For true knowledge proposes a fifth conclusion which asserts that the proportion of velocities in motions follows the proportion of the force of the motor to the force of the thing moved." The formulation here is inexact,[19] but Bradwardine's meaning is clear,

19. The passage reads this way not only in the printed text but also in the manuscripts.

as the subsequent passage makes apparent. Taken literally, his statement does not make sense, since the velocity, not the ratio of velocities, is determined by the ratio of force to resistance. What Bradwardine actually means to say is that the ratio of velocities depends on the "proportion of the proportions of the motive force to the force of the thing moved" *(proportio proportionum potentiae motoris ad potentiam rei motae).*

Thus changes in velocity arise from changes in the ratio of force to resistance; this is the great discovery that Bradwardine claims to have made. The rather surprised modern reader immediately wonders what is really new about this discovery. Does it not say exactly the same thing as the third incorrect opinion, only in a somewhat different form? This apparent difficulty may be the reason why Bradwardine's theory has been ignored up to now by modern research, even though it was announced with considerable fanfare and played an essential role in late scholastic natural philosophy.

For Bradwardine, the statement that velocity varies with the ratio of force to resistance has an entirely different meaning. In the first place, the sentence means what it literally says: a twofold increase in velocity corresponds to a doubling of the proportion of force to resistance, a threefold increase to a trebling of the proportion, and so on. In other words, if the proportion of motive force to resistance increases twofold, threefold, or fivefold, a twofold, threefold, or fivefold increase in velocity ensues. But the crucial point is this: when Bradwardine speaks of doubling and trebling a proportion, he does not mean multiplication by two or three, as in the case of simple quantities. Instead, as he explains in the introductory chapter, he means a twofold or threefold multiplication of the proportion by itself, which is the same as squaring it or raising it to the third power.[20]

---

20. This terminology can be explained as follows. The basic assumption is the so-called rule of the interposed middle *(medium interpositum)*, which can be written in modern symbols $\frac{a}{c} = \frac{a}{b} \cdot \frac{b}{c}$, or more generally in the form $\frac{a}{n} = \frac{a}{b} \cdot \frac{b}{c} \cdot \frac{c}{d} \cdots \frac{m}{n}$. Thus any proportion can be

Thus the essence of Bradwardine's discovery is that squaring the proportion of force to resistance means doubling the velocity, and raising the proportion to the third, fourth, or fifth power entails a threefold, fourfold, or fivefold increase in velocity. Conversely, a twofold increase in velocity presupposes squaring the force and resistance, a threefold increase means cubing them, and so forth. Analogously, the square root[21] corresponds to half the velocity, the cubic root to one third the velocity, and so on. In modern terms, Bradwardine's functional equation relating force and resistance to velocity defines a logarithmic dependence that can be written in symbols as follows: $V = \log \dfrac{F}{R}$ (where V = velocity, F = motive force, and R = resistance). This equation works because operations of multiplication and division on the left side correspond to raising to powers and taking roots on the right: $a \cdot V = \log \left(\dfrac{F}{R} \right)^a$. This solution also avoids the complications arising from the prohibition of a "ratio of equality or lesser inequality." There is no danger that the quotient of force and resistance will become less than or equal

---

expanded into such components in any way desired. Now, in the case in which $\dfrac{a}{b} = \dfrac{b}{c}$ (say $\dfrac{8}{4} = \dfrac{4}{2}$), one can say that the proportion $\dfrac{a}{c}$ contains the proportion $\dfrac{a}{b}$ twice, or that it is the double *(dupla, duplex,* or *duplicata)* of it ($\dfrac{8}{2} = \dfrac{8}{4} \cdot \dfrac{4}{2} = \dfrac{8}{4} \cdot \dfrac{8}{4} = \dfrac{4}{2} \cdot \dfrac{4}{2}$). The following rule applies to the general case: "The proportion composed of a major and a minor is greater than the double of the minor and less than the double of the major." Thus if $\dfrac{9}{2}$ is expanded into $\dfrac{9}{5} \cdot \dfrac{5}{2}$, then in fact $\dfrac{9}{2}$ is greater than $\left(\dfrac{9}{5} \right)^2$ and less than $\left(\dfrac{5}{2} \right)^2$. Correspondingly, the multiplication of proportions (fractions) is universally called "addition," and division is called "subtraction". . . .

21. Or the *medietas* of the corresponding proportion. The word *medietas* when applied to fractions always means the square root. This terminology, which was used everywhere in the fourteenth century, has caused numerous misunderstandings.

to one as a result of changes in velocity, since the mathematical operations no longer involve multiplication and division but rather powers and roots. The n-th root of an improper fraction is itself always an improper fraction and thus never less than or equal to one. The value of the quotient will therefore of necessity always be greater than one.[22]

Bradwardine's functional equation, however, is not consistent with the actual content of Aristotle's text. The general rule that Bradwardine rejects as the third opinion is undoubtedly the one that Aristotle had in mind. In any case, Aristotle confined his analysis to a series of specific cases and never formulated a general law. But it is characteristic of Bradwardine that he does not ask whether his newly discovered function represents a correct inductive generalization of Aristotle's specific rules, but rather the opposite: Are Aristotle's rules valid; are they in fact correct solutions to the problem, even though they are not expressed in a general form? Is it really true that doubling the force or halving the resistance always produces twice the velocity? Bradwardine answers these questions in the *conclusiones* of the third chapter as follows. Aristotle's rules are only correct in one special case, when the ratio of force to resistance is 2:1, since then both multiplying the proportion by two and by itself (that is, squaring it) give the same result. For all other ratios Aristotle's rules do not apply, since the velocity that results when the force is doubled will always be either larger or smaller than twice the previous velocity.[23]

22. [Supplementary comment from the 2d ed. of *Vorläufer*, p. 326:] I have given another derivation of Bradwardine's formula that is simpler and perhaps clearer in *Metaphysische Hintergründe der spätscholastischen Naturphilosophie* (Rome: Edizioni di Storia e Letteratura, 1955), pp. 374–75. Cf. also *Zwischen Philosophie und Mechanik* (Rome: Edizioni di Storia e Letteratura, 1958), p. 240 ff.

The amazement and surprise that greeted my interpretation of Bradwardine's law when this chapter was first published (in *Divus Thomas* 24 [1946]: 147–66) have since subsided, and now this interpretation is generally recognized and accepted as correct.

23. . . . Let me clarify these rather complicated rules with a sample calculation. Suppose that the ratio of force to resistance is 3:2 (i.e., less than 2:1) and that the force is doubled. Then the velocity will be deter-

Bradwardine's theory does nothing to change the original basic principle of dynamics, according to which velocity is determined by the ratio of force to resistance. What it does do is replace the notion of simple proportionality between velocity and the ratio of force to resistance with a more complicated pattern of dependence.

The solution is in fact complicated, but strictly speaking one cannot say that it is wrong. From the standpoint of modern physics, the whole of scholastic-Aristotelian mechanics is "wrong" because acceleration, not velocity, is determined by the relationship between force and resistance. Thus, any function based on Aristotelian assumptions would be misguided. But that is not the point. Bradwardine, like all his contemporaries, believed that Aristotle's physical theory was correct, and he attempted to discover a formula that would apply for all values of the variables and also satisfy all the conditions. And in this he was successful.

---

mined by the ratio 6:2. But doubling the velocity corresponds to squaring the proportion: $(\frac{3}{2})^2 = \frac{9}{4}$. Now, since $\frac{6}{2}$ is larger than $\frac{9}{4}$, in this case doubling the force results in more than twice the original velocity. If, on the other hand, the ratio of force to resistance is less than 2:1, the reverse is true.

Four:

THE SIGNIFICANCE OF THE
THEORY OF IMPETUS
FOR SCHOLASTIC NATURAL
PHILOSOPHY

The theory of impetus has long been regarded as one of the major achievements of late scholastic natural philosophy. It has also been one of the major points of contention in the debate over the true relationship between medieval and modern science. As Anneliese Maier indicates at the beginning of this essay, the question is whether the theory of impetus in any way prefigured the law of inertia, that cornerstone of classical dynamics that achieved its standard formulation in Newton's first law: "Every body remains in a state of rest or of uniform rectilinear motion until it is forced to change its state by impressed forces."

Many writers have discussed the theory of impetus, but few, if any, have done so as authoritatively as Anneliese Maier. Pierre Duhem first drew attention to the theory in his Études sur Léonard de Vinci, *3 vols. (Paris: Hermann, 1906–13), but his interpretations are not always reliable. Maier's detailed and comprehensive study,* Die Impetustheorie der Scholastik *(Vienna: Schroll, 1940), an expanded version of which was published in* Zwei Grundprobleme der scholastischen Naturphilosophie, *2d ed. (Rome: Edizioni di Storia e Letteratura, 1951), is still the standard work on the topic. Supplementary discussions of various special problems were published in other volumes of the* Studien. *(See footnote 4 below for details.)*

The article translated here, "Die naturphilosophische Bedeutung der scho-lastischen Impetustheorie," originally appeared in Scholastik 30 (1955): *321–43 and was reprinted in* Ausgehendes Mittelalter, vol. 1 (Rome: Edizioni di Storia e Letteratura, 1964), pp. 353–79. *It contains Maier's mature assessment of the nature of impetus and its relationship to the modern concept of inertia. It also has an expanded discussion of the inertial tendency of bodies to return to a state of rest mentioned in chapter 2 that Maier in this essay calls* inclinatio ad quietem. *The translation follows the text in* Ausgehendes Mittelalter. *I have omitted the last two paragraphs on Galileo and impetus theory because chapter 5 examines this topic in greater detail.*

Among scholars actually familiar with the relevant sources differences of opinion still exist on the true interpretation of the scholastic theory of impetus. Among those less acquainted with the subject, one encounters a combination of misunderstanding and bias. The question that has come up for discussion repeatedly and has attracted an unusual amount of interest even in wider circles is whether, and to what extent, the late scholastic explanation of inertial motion (which, following Buridan's terminology, is usually called the theory of impetus) not only prepared the way for but also actually anticipated the law of inertia of classical mechanics.

There is no doubt that it *prepared the way* for the law of inertia. The theory of impetus occupies an important and enduring place in the history of natural philosophy and physics as an independent stage of development between Aristotelianism and classical mechanics. In this role of connecting link it furnished the illustrious founders of modern science with the point of departure for the development of their new theories. But this late scholastic theory has frequently been regarded as something more, namely, a true *anticipation* of the system of mechanics based on the law of inertia.[1]

1. This view was advocated by Pierre Duhem, who first drew attention to the scholastic theory of impetus in his *Études sur Léonard de Vinci*, 3 vols. (Paris: Hermann, 1906–13). Since then, the problem has been discussed repeatedly.

The issue is this: did the natural philosophers of the fourteenth century formulate, either explicitly or implicitly, a theory that represents in their language and within the framework of their cosmological assumptions a law analogous to the law of inertia of classical physics? Did they, in other words, advance an interpretation that in any way implies or logically entails that uniform motion (that is, motion in a straight line at a constant velocity) will continue forever if it encounters no resistance? From the outset, however, we must recognize that we are only dealing with an *analogue* to the law of inertia, not an exact parallel to it. An exact parallel is out of the question, since late scholastic thinkers assumed that uniform motion is caused by a special kind of motive force called *impetus,* while modern mechanics postulates that uniform motion does not require any force to make it continue, but instead persists of its own accord because of the inertia of the mass involved. Moreover, whereas classical physics from the start employs the notion of an infinite space where such infinite rectilinear motion can conceivably take place, scholastic philosophers thought only in terms of a closed universe of finite dimension; for them, circular motion by necessity takes the place of linear motion in any discussion of eternal movement. The only remaining point of comparison between the two systems is regular motion, that is, motion of constant velocity that lasts forever if no change occurs in the stipulated conditions. Thus the question becomes, Does scholastic impetus theory admit the possibility of such motion?

Buridan makes certain statements that can be interpreted as affirming such a possibility if they are considered in isolation, without regard to the context in which they occur and without reference to the assumptions that make them intelligible. The most important of these statements is found in a passage in his commentary on the *Metaphysics;* it in fact appears to articulate something like a scholastic law of inertia. We shall see later on what a close reading of this passage reveals, but first one more basic observation must be made. All discussions of impetus theory labor under one major difficulty that appears every time an attempt is made to reach a deeper understanding: we do not possess the concepts and terminology necessary to reproduce the ideas of late scholastic thinkers with any exactitude. Impetus is neither a force, nor a form of energy, nor momentum in the modern sense; it shares something with all these other concepts, but it is identical with none of them. Thus we lack the tools to describe precisely what the concept of impetus really means. Every expression that we might employ possesses a definite, technical meaning in the terminology of present-day physics, and unfortunately no generally understandable language of modern natural philosophy as yet exists. It must, therefore, be emphasized from the outset that in what follows terms such as force, energy, and inertial resistance are used only in an approximate sense and consequently must always be taken with a grain of salt.

The problem of detached motion *(motus separatus)*, which led in the fourteenth century to the formulation of impetus theory, arises in scholastic philosophy from Aristotle's universally accepted and indisputable principle *omne quod movetur ab aliquo movetur:* all motion presupposes a motive force, a *virtus* or *vis motrix*, as its cause. Motion continues only as long as the motive force exists, and it ceases at the very moment when this force is extinguished. There is no motion without a motive force. But action at a distance, that is, the operation of a mover on an object spatially removed from it, is excluded as impossible. What, then, causes the motion of an arrow or a stone in flight?

In the course of the history of philosophy many answers have been given to this question. Aristotle himself discusses a few and rejects them, including the so-called theory of *antiperistasis,* which seeks to explain the process by a kind of swirling motion in the air. He comes to the following conclusion. The original mover (the *proiciens*) conveys to the medium a part of its own motive force in "waves" of decreasing strength, so that the air in the direction of flight is, as it were, charged with a progressively decreasing force that extends for a certain distance. The projectile continues to move after its separation from the *proiciens* as long as this (quasilinear) force field persists, and it moves with decreasing velocity in conformity with the decreasing strength of the motive force in the individual "waves" of air. This latter notion follows from another fundamental principle of scholastic-Aristotelian mechanics, which requires that the magnitude of a velocity be directly proportional to the magnitude of the motive force and inversely proportional to the magnitude of the resistance that the motive force must overcome. Albertus Magnus formulates the principle in this fashion: "Every motion arises from the victory of the motive force over the object moved; and when the force operates, it is necessary that the passive potentiality of the thing moved be proportional to the force."[2] Velocity is a function of the quotient of force and resistance, and when, as in our case, the resistance remains unchanged, the velocity depends exclusively on the magnitude of the motive force.[3]

Moreover, yet another principle of scholastic-Aristotelian natural philosophy finds expression in this explanation of projectile motion. The projectile, once it is separated from the original mover, is moved by the force field at a rate that corresponds to the continually decreasing motive force in such a way that at every point all the available force is used up—since after the projectile passes by there is of course no more force left. In other words, it is moved in such a way that the motive force imparted to the medium is *transformed* into the motion of the projectile. This is the key point. Obviously the Aristotelian concept of motive force contains a concrete element that can only be evoked imperfectly by the modern term "force." It resembles more a kind of energy that is transformed into motion and used up in the process. This idea is important for the correct understanding of impetus theory.

Early on it was recognized that Aristotle's explanation of detached motion has serious weaknesses. Already in late antiquity Johannes Philoponus (or Grammaticus) attempted to revise it using substantially the same approach as the later theory of impetus. The same idea is again found in the writings of Islamic Aristotelians,

2. Albertus Magnus, *Physica* VIII, tract. II, cap. 6. ["Omnis motus provenit ex virtutis moventis victoria super mobile, et cum illa virtus movet, oportet potentiam passivam eius, quod movetur, sibi esse proportionalem."]

3. Aristotle assumed that the relationship was one of simple proportionality, whereas in the fourteenth century a much more complicated function was proposed. But the fundamental principle that the velocity depends on the quotient of motive force and resistance remained unchanged.

especially Avicenna. It appears that Avicenna founded a whole school of thought that can be traced down to the seventeenth century and that parallels the Western development of impetus theory. Nevertheless, no lines of dependence or influence can be demonstrated. These matters cannot, however, be pursued any further here, since the topic to be considered is the fourteenth-century scholastic theory of impetus.[4]

The first thinker to state the theory of impetus in a detailed and thorough fashion was the Italian Franciscan and Scotist, Franciscus de Marchia. He did so in the course of his lectures on the *Sentences* given at Paris during the academic year 1319–20, as we know from a summary *(reportatio)* of the lectures preserved in several manuscripts. The man who became the chief exponent of impetus theory was Jean Buridan, who addressed the problem explicitly in his commentary on the *Physics* about a decade after Marchia and developed the idea of impetus into a real theory. His critique of Aristotle's solution is no longer predominately speculative in nature, as was Marchia's, but is instead based on the facts of experience (which sometimes resemble the data of experiments) and upon undisguised considerations of natural philosophy and physics. But the resulting theory is essentially the same in both cases: at the moment of separation the thrower imparts a secondary motive force not to the medium but to the projectile itself, and it is this residual force (Marchia calls it *vis derelicta,* Buridan *vis impressa* or *impetus*) that causes the subsequent motion of the detached projectile. An analogous idea explains why the rotation of water wheels, grindstones, and tops persists after the external motive force has been removed. Such

---

4. For the history of impetus see *Zwei Grundprobleme der scholastischen Naturphilosophie*, 2d ed. (Rome: Edizioni di Storia e Letteratura, 1951), p. 113 ff; for various special problems see, in addition, *Die Vorläufer Galileis* (Rome: Edizioni di Storia e Letteratura, 1949), p. 132 ff., *An der Grenze von Scholastik und Naturphilosophie*, 2d ed. (Rome: Edizioni di Storia e Letteratura, 1952), p. 199 ff., *Metaphysische Hintergründe der spätscholastischen Naturphilosophie* (Rome: Edizioni di Storia e Letteratura, 1955), p. 264 ff. and 362 ff. [and *Zwischen Philosophie und Mechanik* (Rome: Edizioni di Storia e Letteratura, 1958), pp. 343–73.]

motion also arises from an impetus, but in this instance it operates circularly, not linearly. In contrast to later mechanical theory, scholastic natural philosophy sees no essential difference between the two phenomena. Impetus is regarded as a motive force that produces the same kind of motion as the original mover, be it upward, downward, sideways, or circular.

In Buridan's writings the theory, now fully developed, reaches its true highpoint. Nicole Oresme, Buridan's famous student, makes several interesting distinctions, but (as will be seen further on) he interprets the concept of impetus in a fundamentally different way than Buridan. In any case, his reinterpretation attracted hardly any supporters. The natural philosophers of the second half of the fourteenth century, of whom the most important were Albert of Saxony, who subsequently founded the University of Vienna, and Marsilius of Inghen, who was later the first rector of Heidelberg, follow Buridan exclusively. Yet they were by and large content to present the theory in a clear and organized fashion and to refine a few concepts without adding anything new. Their chief accomplishment consisted in transmitting the theory to later centuries, when the writings of Albert and Marsilius were much more widely read than those of Buridan and Oresme.

But what is the true nature of this impetus that fourteenth-century philosophers used to explain inertial motion? Buridan himself asks, "What sort of thing is impetus?" This remained the central problem, and it was discussed repeatedly without ever receiving an entirely satisfactory solution.

In order to understand the problem clearly, let us go back a number of years before Buridan's time. Already in the thirteenth century an unusual early version of the theory of impetus appears in the writings of the great Franciscan philosopher, Peter John Olivi. This theory is found in his questions on the second book of the *Sentences*, which have been edited by B. Jansen.[5] There Olivi

---

5. Questions 23–31, especially no. 29, in vol. 1 of Jansen's ed. Jansen had previously drawn attention to this theory in an essay in the *Philosophisches Jahrbuch der Görresgesellschaft* 23 (1920): 137 ff. I have long thought, and still do, that it must be interpreted somewhat differently than it is by Jansen, who frankly regards Olivi as the first advocate of the true theory of impetus.

reports that certain thinkers *(quidam)* have advanced the theory that projectile motion results from the action of a tendency *(inclinatio)*, image *(species)*, or likeness *(similitudo)* that the mover imparts to the projectile and that then causes the projectile to continue to move in the mover's absence. This tendency, however, is not a true motive force; it is only the image or likeness of one and does not possess the full nature of a motive force. Whether Olivi himself actually agreed with this theory or whether he only intended to report it is not at issue here. For our purposes it is only important that such an explanation of projectile motion was given. It says that the motion of a projectile is produced by an image *(species)* that is basically similar in nature to the sensible species *(species sensibiles)* that produce perception in the sense organs. Thus this precursor of impetus is something that does not correspond, even approximately, to any later physical concept.

In another work[6] Olivi energetically rejects and refutes this same theory, and in doing so he shows himself to be in this regard, as in many others, a precursor of Ockham.[7] He shows that local motion cannot possibly be produced by such an image or likeness, and then, since no other form of efficient causality is left to be considered, he concludes that this motion has no cause and therefore cannot be a truly real, "absolute" factor. It is simply a "mode of being situated" *(modus se habendi)* or, in modern terminology, a *state* of the moving object. This is one of the places, and a very early one at that, where a scholastic thinker came close to discovering the law of inertia, although here the argument has nothing to do with the theory of impetus. Basically, this definition of mo-

6. In a *quaestio* located in codex Vat. Borgh. 322 (fol. 127v–129v) that reads: "Whether local motion signifies anything absolute beyond the object that is moved in place." In my catalogue of the Borghese manuscripts (*Codices Burghesiani Bibliothecae Vaticanae* [Vatican City: Biblioteca apostolica vaticana, 1952]), I put a question mark after the attribution of this *quaestio* to Olivi, but I am nevertheless convinced that it is certainly his at least in content, if not in the form in which it has come down to us (Cf. *Metaphysische Hintergründe*, p. 355 ff.).

7. For the relationship between Olivi and Ockham see *Ausgehendes Mittelalter*, vol. 1 (Rome: Edizioni di Storia e Letteratura, 1964), p. 193 ff., and *Metaphysische Hintergründe*, chap. III,1 (and elsewhere).

tion is exactly the same as the one implicit in the law of inertia: motion is a state, a real mode of being of the moving object that needs no special force to continue to exist. Of course the idea that such motion could last indefinitely was unthinkable for Olivi because of his understanding of the concept of time. Thus he never took that last step that would have actually allowed him to formulate the true law of inertia.

Whether and to what extent the *quaestio* in which Olivi presents these ideas attracted attention and influenced other thinkers cannot be determined. Nevertheless, it is tempting to ask whether William of Ockham was familiar with it. He himself gave two different explanations for detached motion, the second of which clearly represents a modification of the first and can undoubtedly be regarded as his "real" opinion. Originally he explained the motion of a detached projectile very simply as the result of a virtual connection *(simultas virtualis)* between the projector and the projectile, that is, as the result of the operation of the original mover at a distance. Although Ockham completely rejected all causal effects produced by the action of images *(species),* especially in the case of sense perception, it is entirely correct to say that he adopted basically the same approach to projectile motion that Olivi proposed in his commentary on the *Sentences;* only here, as in the case of other phenomena that are explained analogously, he avoided the use of images by replacing them with a direct causal connection operating at a distance. In his second explanation Ockham rejected, just as Olivi did in the other question, the need for any special cause for detached motion at all, but for the opposite reason. Motion is not something absolute, something real in and of itself that differs from the object and the places it occupies (or the qualities or the quantities it acquires); hence no special cause needs to be sought for motion in the special case of a detached projectile. Unlike Olivi, however, Ockham did not develop this position into a theory of motion that could be regarded as approximating the basic intent of the law of inertia.[8] He was too preoccupied with his attempt to eliminate

8. H. Lange (*Geschichte der Grundlagen der Physik,* vol. 1 [Freiburg/Munich: K. Alber, 1954], p. 159) cites (in German) a passage that he attributes to Ockham, in which the law of inertia is formulated in a most unequivocal

the idea of motion as a formal, objective factor to offer another, positive ontological interpretation of it. Only in the reaction against Ockham's views found in the writings of Buridan do we encounter a new attempt to describe motion as a kind of state of the moving body.[9] Buridan's approach, however, is completely different from Olivi's: motion is not a mode of being of the moving object but a qualitylike factor that inheres in it. This idea, too, could have given rise to a theory analogous to the law of inertia, since it would have been easy to conclude that such a factor can, like any other quality, continue to exist by itself without any external cause. But instead of taking the decisive step in this direction, Buridan conceived the problem of inertial motion in another fashion and solved it with his theory of impetus. Further on I will consider its relationship to the law of inertia.

First, however, some further observations must be made about the concept of impetus as it was developed by Franciscus de Marchia, who, as I said earlier, was the first one really to advocate this theory. His definition of the *vis derelicta* that moves projectiles reflects his belief that Aristotle provided a fundamentally correct solution that only needed to be corrected on a single point. In his view, it is true that projectile motion results from a transmitted force, not from a swirling motion of the air, or from its gravity or levity, or from the form of the heavens *(forma caeli)*. Aristotle was only mistaken about the object to which this force is transmitted; it is not the medium that receives the *vis derelicta*, but the projectile

---

fashion. The passage stands in quotation marks, but there is no indication of where the author found it. It does not, in any case, derive from any genuine work by Ockham, who never made such a statement (and never could have). Moreover, to me it appears more than doubtful that Ockham's concept of motion could be construed in a transcendental-logical sense that anticipates Kant's ideas, an interpretation that Lange, following G. Martin, advocates. The surviving texts do not support such an interpretation, and when considering scholastic authors, one should especially avoid reading too much "between the lines."

9. For Buridan's concept of motion and his opposition to Ockham's see *Die Vorläufer Galileis*, p. 19 ff. [translated in chap. 1 above] and *Metaphysische Hintergründe*, p. 350 ff.

itself. Otherwise, Marchia's description of this force is entirely consistent with Aristotle's ideas. Aristotle conjectured that the force in
question becomes weaker from one "wave" of air to the next; correspondingly, Marchia postulates that the motive force transmitted to
the projectile gradually decreases, although in a temporal rather
than a spatial sense, and after a while disappears all by itself. It is
therefore a "sort of intermediate form" *(forma quasi media)* between
the "purely successive form" that motion is *(forma simpliciter successiva)* and a "purely permanent quality" *(forma simpliciter permanens)*.
It is something that lasts for a short period of time *(per modicum
tempus)* and then disappears, regardless of whether any external
forces are present to destroy it. A motive force of this kind cannot
last for very long because of the imperfection of its mode of being
(propter imperfectionem suae entitatis), just as images in the eye, which
are caused by lighted objects, do not have any permanent existence,
but only last for a time and then vanish by themselves.

Buridan's opinion on this point, however, is fundamentally different. He asks, "What sort of thing is impetus" *(quae res est ille
impetus)*, and he answers that it is "something permanent by nature"
(res naturae permanentis). He gives this answer in the form of three
propositions. The first of these is undoubtedly meant to counter
Ockham's second explanation: impetus is not identical with local
motion itself but is its cause, and nothing can be its own cause. But
impetus is also, generally speaking, not a "pure successiveness" *(res
pure successiva)*; that is, it is not simply a flux, because (as he has said
elsewhere, Buridan adds) it would once again have to be motion, and
the same difficulties would arise as in the previous solution. Buridan
had in fact already demonstrated in another discussion that local
motion is not only a successive *process*, but also a real "successive
thing" *(res successiva)*, a flux that to a certain extent inheres in the
moving object as an accident. It is, as mentioned earlier, a kind of
state. Thus Buridan's point is that impetus is different not only from
motion as Ockham defines it, that is, from motion as a mere process,[10] but also from motion as he himself conceives it, that is, from

10. For Ockham the concept "motion" is merely a name, a substantive
that takes the place of the declarative sentence "something is moved."

motion as a state. From this proposition Buridan could have developed his concept of motion in a way that would have led him to formulate the law of inertia, but he followed another course instead.

The third proposition states that impetus is actually "something permanent by nature and distinct from the local motion with which the projectile is moved" *(res naturae permanentis distincta a motu locali quo illud proiectum movetur).* And in all likelihood, Buridan adds, it is a quality whose essence is to move the body in which it inheres. Furthermore, this quality can apparently be impeded, diminished, and destroyed just like motion and by the same resistance or contrary tendency *(inclinatio contraria).*

Thus in Buridan's opinion, the cause of detached motion is a truly real accident of the projectile that is probably a motive quality like gravity or the force of a magnet, that is, a quality that produces local motion. It is not just a "sort of intermediate form" with a limited life span, as Franciscus de Marchia supposed, and even less so a mere image or likeness of the original motive force, as Olivi said. It is instead a true quality like the original force that has complete physical reality[11] and a permanent existence. Of course, this does not mean that it is imperishable or incorruptible; on the contrary, like all real accidents it is capable of being destroyed by an opposing agent *(a contrario agente).* And since impetus is probably a motive quality in the strict sense, then the factors that can destroy it should be conceived correspondingly. They must be the same ones that operate against local motion itself, namely, external resistances and those internal tendencies by which the moving object opposes the mover.

In the writings of Nicole Oresme impetus takes on a somewhat different character. He believes that Buridan's theory has to be modified to account for a phenomenon supposedly confirmed by

---

11. Buridan's impetus is absolutely not an "immaterial force" as H. Lange *(Geschichte der Grundlagen der Physik,* 1:160) supposes, but rather a material, substantial one. Furthermore, the expression *vis immateriata* that Lange employs in this connection (it does not occur in fourteenth-century terminology) would denote just that: a force that has entered *into* the material and is hence a material, not an immaterial, force.

experience whose validity many scholastic thinkers accepted on the basis of a misunderstood passage in Aristotle. This is the apparent acceleration of a projectile at the beginning of its flight. An object was thought to reach its highest velocity only some time after being released by the thrower, rather than begin to slow down immediately. Buridan declared that he had never made such an observation and was uncertain if it was indeed correct; in any case, he does not take the hypothesis into account in his impetus theory. Oresme, on the other hand, constructs his theory entirely on the basis of this illusory problem and therefore concludes that impetus must be regarded as the cause not of constant velocity, but rather of constant acceleration. This concept of force is closely related to Newton's formulation. But Oresme's theory never progressed beyond the initial stages, which contained numerous uncertainties and inconsistencies, so that his modification of impetus theory attracted little attention.

Oresme also deviates from Buridan's theory on another point. He gives up the idea that impetus is permanent in nature and concludes, as Franciscus de Marchia did, that it dies out by itself after a while, regardless of whether any destructive forces are present. Most later advocates of impetus theory shared this opinion.[12] Only a few thinkers, especially Albert of Saxony, remained convinced of Buridan's assertion that impetus is permanent in nature.

It is, of course, out of the question to suppose that an impetus defined as a temporary force might constitute the discovery of the law of inertia in any way whatsoever. Only Buridan's version of the concept allows such conjectures. Moreover, as I said earlier, there exists a passage in his writings that in fact seems to support such an interpretation. It occurs in his commentary on the *Metaphysics* in

12. This is not to imply that later thinkers actually derived this notion from Oresme or even that they could have; his theory of impetus had far too small an effect for that. The idea of a self-subsiding impetus was simply considered by almost all supporters of the theory to be more obvious, more natural, and more evident than the assumption of a permanent motive quality.

connection with the question "Whether there are as many celestial motions as there are intelligences" and the passage reads:

> You know that many maintain that a projectile, after leaving the thrower, is moved by impetus imparted by the thrower and moves as long as the impetus remains stronger than the resistance; and that the impetus would last forever if it were not diminished and destroyed by the opposing resistance or by the tendency to contrary motion.[13]

This passage really seems to present an analogue to the law of the conservation of motion within the framework of impetus theory. Of course, Buridan does not say that the motion of a detached projectile would last forever if there were no resistance, but he does say that the force that causes this motion would last forever under the stipulated conditions, and this appears to be the same thing. But is it really the same?

First of all, it must be noted that the conclusions that Buridan draws from this remark and that prompt him to make it in the first place do not concern terrestrial motions but rather celestial motions. The passage continues:

> And in celestial motions there is no opposing resistance; therefore when God, at the Creation, moved each sphere of the heavens with just the velocity he wished, he [then] ceased to move them himself, and since then those motions have lasted forever due to the impetus impressed on those spheres.

13. Buridan, *Metaphysica* XII, qu. 9: ["Utrum quot sunt motus caelestes, tot sint intelligentiae." The passage reads: "Vos scitis quod multi ponunt, quod proiectum post exitum a proiciente movetur ab impetu dato a proiciente et movetur quamdiu durat impetus fortior quam resistentia; et in infinitum duraret impetus, nisi diminueretur et corrumperetur a resistente contrario vel ab inclinante ad contrarium motum."] The same idea is also presented, although in a less precise form, in the commentary on the *Physics* in the context of the interpretation of impetus theory (Buridan, *Physica* VIII, qu. 12). [The passage continues in the next paragraph: "Et in motibus caelestibus nullum est resistens contrarium, ideo cum in creatione mundi Deus quamlibet sphaeram movit qua velocitate voluit, ipse cessavit a movendo, et per impetum illis sphaeris impressum semper postea duraverunt illi motus."]

Buridan means to say that it is possible to explain celestial motions solely on the basis of mechanical forces, without any resort to intelligences. This idea represents a rather daring hypothesis, not only from the standpoint of the theological powers *(domini theologici)* to whom he cautiously entrusts the final decision on the matter, but from the physical standpoint as well. This topic will be discussed later. For the time being, it is enough to establish that Buridan had in mind celestial and not terrestrial motions when he formulated his "law of inertia."

But is it not possible for the statement to be valid for terrestrial mechanics even though Buridan does not explicitly say so? Before this question can be answered, one has to determine what resistances can work in opposition to impetus and how they might be eliminated. Scholastic thinkers customarily distinguished between the external resistances that operate to impede a moving body and the internal resistances that the moving body itself sets up against the mover. In practice, the only external resistance that affects impetus is the friction of the medium, which can easily be disregarded. The friction of whatever supporting surface is involved was generally not taken into account. Thus the external impediments do not present any difficulties. The internal ones consist of the natural tendencies of every material body to offer a resistance, an *inclinatio contraria,* to every violently induced motion. Principal among them is gravity: scholastic-Aristotelian philosophy explained the free fall of a heavy body not as the result of the action of some external force, but rather as the result of an innate tendency, the body's attempt to return to its "natural place," namely, to the center of the world, which coincides with the center of the earth. In theory, therefore, this tendency cannot really be disregarded, since it pertains to the essence and nature of all heavy bodies, but in certain circumstances it can be excluded for all practical purposes. This is the case if the motion takes place on a level surface or, to be more exact, on the surface of the earth at a constant distance from its center. A rolling ball or a cart that is pushed and then allowed to move on its own is an example of detached motion in which gravitational resistance is in fact excluded.

There is, however, yet another kind of internal resistance that opposes impetus and attempts to destroy it. A body at rest offers resistance to every motive force that tries to set it in motion: both scholastic and classical mechanics agree on this point. But in the case of a body already in motion their viewpoints differ. Let us for a moment turn our attention away from the detached motion of an arrow in flight or of a rolling ball and examine conjoint motion *(motus coniunctus)*, in which the mover and the thing moved are in contact (and both in motion). An example of this is a cart that is pushed or pulled by Socrates or by a horse. In classical mechanics an object like this in a state of uniform motion offers no resistance to its mover, whereas it does so in scholastic theory, and the magnitude of the resistance is exactly the same as for an object at rest. This is the fundamental principle of all scholastic-Aristotelian mechanics. *Omne quod movetur ab aliquo movetur:* all motion is at all times something produced by an external agent. Every material body in its natural and characteristic state is at rest. It is therefore always virtually at rest, even when it is moved violently, and consequently the mover must continually overcome its inertial resistance. This inertial resistance always remains constant, whether the body is in a state of rest or of motion.

On the other hand, those fourteenth-century scholastic natural philosophers who were starting to take empirical evidence into account could not ignore the fact that "apparently" less force is required to maintain the motion of a moving cart than to set into motion one that is at rest. But this observation was either rejected as an illusion[14] or explained away somehow. One such explanation conjectured that the motive force, as it begins to act on an object at rest, does not affect every part of the object immediately, so that the application *(applicatio)* of the force only occurs gradually. This, then, accounts for both the initial acceleration of the object and the "illusion" that more energy is needed to set it in motion. In any case, scholastic philosophers believed that a cart being pushed or pulled by Socrates offers him a resistance that is in essence an attempt at every instant to restore itself to a state of rest. (In contrast, according to the law of inertia of classical mechanics, the cart attempts to preserve a state of uniform motion.) Now, the same precepts that apply to conjoint motion *(motus coniunctus)* of course also apply to

14. There is a very clear example of this in *Die Vorläufer Galileis,* p. 152.

detached motion *(motus separatus)* and, in particular, to the resistance offered by an object in flight or by a rolling ball to the impetus causing its motion.

Later fourteenth-century natural philosophers labeled this inertial resistance of a moving body the "tendency toward rest" *(inclinatio ad quietem).* [15] Nicole Oresme was the first author to present the concept in a completely clear fashion. Buridan did not yet have it in an explicit form. It is unfortunate that Oresme's commentary on the *Physics* is lost, since in it he directly addressed the topic of impetus theory and probably this topic too. Nevertheless, there are still enough passages in the works that have survived to enable us to reconstruct his thinking. Already in his *Questions on the Sphere of Johannes de Sacrobosco,* which was probably written very early in his career, we find this very interesting remark: "every moving object that offers resistance to some mover tends toward rest or toward contrary motion." [16] And the same idea appears again in his Latin *Questions on De caelo et mundo,* which is also a relatively early work. Oresme means to show that the motions of the heavens take place without any resistance, and he does so by introducing the following consideration: "The heavens do not offer resistance (to their mover); this is immediately obvious because then the heavens would tend toward rest or contrary motion and if this were so, then they would be moved violently." [17] And again, in the same context: "Further-

15. This "tendency toward rest," which I was the first to call attention to, was received with considerable amazement and skepticism. Once I was even accused of more or less inventing this inertial resistance. For this reason, I will cite a number of passages here that may help to dispel these doubts and objections. (Cf. also *Metaphysische Hintergründe,* p. 363 ff.)

16. ["Omne mobile quod resistit alicui motori, inclinatur ad quietem vel ad motum oppositum."] Oresme adds: "This is apparent, because if you examine it well, resistance does not seem to be anything else." A manuscript of these questions is in codex Vat. lat. 2185, fol. 71r–77v. (The quotation comes from qu. 9, fol. 75r.)

17. These questions, too, are only available in manuscript. I used (in microfilm) Erfurt Ms. Ampl. Qu. 299; the quotations come from the question "Utrum caelum moveatur sine fatigatione," fol. 27r–v. ["Caelum non resistit (motori) quod statim patet, quia tunc caelum inclinaretur ad quietem vel motum contrarium, et si ita esset, tunc moveretur violente."]

more there is no external resistance, because (the heavens) do not divide a medium as they move like a heavy object does; nor is there internal resistance, because they do not have a·tendency toward contrary motion or rest."[18] These passages reveal indirectly what kinds of resistance are involved in violent terrestrial motion: the external resistance of the medium and an internal resistance made up of two components, the tendency toward contrary motion, that is, gravity, and the tendency toward rest, that is, inertial resistance.

An obvious reference to the passage in Oresme's Latin commentary on *De caelo* appears in the *Questions on De caelo et mundo* of Dominic of Clavasio, a student of both Buridan and Oresme. He too wants to demonstrate that in the case of celestial motions the moving object offers no resistance to the mover: "This is manifest, for if (an intelligence were to produce motion with resistance) it would be because (the heavens) either tend toward rest or toward contrary motion, neither of which can be postulated."[19] Albert of Saxony, too, may be referring to the same passage in Oresme when he writes: "The heavens do not offer resistance to their mover . . . for if they did resist the mover, then they would tend toward rest or toward contrary motion; and if it were so, then the heavens would be moved violently."[20] There is also another passage in Albert's writings in which he explicitly introduces the tendency toward rest

18. ["Etiam non est resistentia extrinseca, quia (caelum) non movetur dividendo medium sicut grave, nec intrinseca, quia non habet inclinationem ad motum oppositum aut quietem."] An analogous statement from Oresme's French commentary on *De caelo et mundo* is cited later in the essay.

19. Lib. II, qu. 1: "Utrum caelum moveatur cum fatigatione et poena." There is a manuscript of these questions in Vat. lat. 2185, fol. 1r–20v. (The quotation is on fol. 13v.) ["Patet, nam si (intelligentia moveret cum resistentia) hoc esset vel quia (caelum) inclinaretur ad quietem vel ad motum oppositum, quod neutrum potest dari."]

20. Albert of Saxony, *De caelo et mundo* (numerous editions, e.g., Venice, 1492), lib. II, qu. 9; he too asks "Utrum caelum moveatur cum poena et fatigatione." ["Caelum non resistit motori . . . nam si resisteret motori, tunc inclinaretur ad quietem vel ad motum contrarium, et si ita esset, tunc caelum moveretur violente."]

as a factor that destroys impetus: "This impetus is destroyed by . . . the tendency of the moving object toward rest."[21]

The term "tendency toward rest" does not appear in the works of earlier writers. Even in Buridan's writings the internal resistance of a moving object is simply called a "contrary tendency" *(inclinatio contraria)*, and no attempt is made to analyze it further. But this is not to say that Oresme was introducing something new when he used the phrase "tendency toward rest." It is rather that here, as in many other cases, he simply went further in his analysis of the concept than other thinkers and explicitly emphasized one aspect that earlier writers had implicitly included in their notion of "the resistance that a moving body offers to the mover." Moreover, he developed the concept generally, not merely with reference to the special case of motion caused by impetus.

In order to convince ourselves of this fact, let us consider once again the ordinary case of conjoint motion, as when an object is pulled or pushed by Socrates. How would scholastic philosophers say that the resistance that this moving object (on a level course) offers to its mover should be measured? There is only one answer to this question, and everyone who examined the problem accepted it: the measure is the weight, the *pondus.* In the seventh book of the *Physics* Aristotle presents certain rules concerning the relationship between force, resistance, and velocity. Whenever commentators on the *Physics* discussed the idea found in these rules of doubling or halving a resistance, they took it entirely for granted that the measure of these differences was the weight of the moving body. This was so even though only horizontal motion was considered, in which case only inertia, and not gravity, comes into play. A similar question arose in the discussion of *maxima:* Is there a maximum weight that Socrates can just barely move or a minimum one that he cannot quite move? Generally speaking, however, commentators considered pulling and pushing motions rather than lifting mo-

---

21. ["Talis impetus corrumpitur per . . . inclinationem ipsius mobilis ad quietem."] Ibid. qu. 14. I cited this passage and the (not entirely clear) context in which it stands in an earlier work (*Zwei Grundprobleme*, p. 269 f.). Here I am only interested in the explicit reference to the "tendency toward rest" as a resistance that destroys impetus.

tions. To put it briefly, scholastic philosophers did not distinguish between inertial and gravitational mass, at least not in their terminology. Oresme was the first one to make this distinction and to recognize clearly that the two internal tendencies of a body in violent motion are both incorporated into the traditional concept of gravity. He makes this point in his French commentary on *De caelo et mundo* in a discussion of the phrase "and the heavens are moved without work or effort."[22] Here he says, "For the reason why such things as men and animals experience work or effort or pain in moving themselves or other heavy things is that *their weight inclines them toward rest or to be moved with some other contrary motion.*" And once again: "But the heavens have neither weight in themselves or outside nor anything else to make them tend toward rest or toward any other motion than their own."

Thus at least as early as Buridan, the tendency to return to a state of rest is a component of the "contrary tendency" of a moving body that its impetus has to overcome, despite the fact that this is not explicitly stated. And this tendency toward rest is, of course, a kind of resistance that cannot be disregarded either in theory or in practice. Thus the precondition for the existence of an impetus of infinite duration that Buridan formulates in his commentary on the *Metaphysics* (that is, the absence of all resistance) cannot be fulfilled, at least not in the case of terrestrial motion.

Nevertheless, let us pursue the question further and ask what would happen if this precondition were fulfilled. If a terrestrial impetus could operate in the absence of all resistance, would an analogue to the law of inertia really be the result? Again the answer is no. In such a case, according to scholastic theory, no mo-

22. *Traité du ciel et du monde*, livre II, chap. 3, ed. A. D. Menut and A. J. Denomy in *Mediaeval Studies*, vols. 3–5 (1941–1943); the quotation is found in vol. 4, p. 174. [Now also in Nicole Oresme, *Le livre du ciel et du monde*, ed. A. D. Menut and A. J. Denomy, trans. A. D. Menut (Madison, Wis.: University of Wisconsin Press, 1968), p. 296. "Car la cause pourquoy telles choses comme sont hommes et bestes, ont labour et travail ou poine en mouvant elles meismes ou autres choses pesantes, est pour ce que pesanteur les encline a reposer ou a estre meues d'autre mouvement aucunement contraire." And, "Mais le ciel n'a ne en soy ne dehors pesanteur ne quelcunque autre chose qui l'encline a repos ou a autre mouvement que le sien."]

tion in the strict sense would occur. Instead there would be a *mutatio,* that is, an instantaneous change of position, rather than a successive process that takes place over time. If the impossible were done and all resistance were removed, then an impetus would produce motion not of infinite duration but of infinite velocity. The basic principle underlying all scholastic mechanics says that velocity is a function of the quotient of force and resistance. Given a certain force, the smaller the resistance is, the greater the resulting velocity will be. And if the magnitude of the resistance tends to zero, the velocity will necessarily become infinite. This conclusion applies generally to every natural force that acts on a spatially extended, physical object or, to use Aristotle's terminology, to every force that exists and operates *in magnitudine.* Only the detached movers *(motores separati)* that move the heavens are not subject to this principle, since the intelligences are spiritual forces that cause motion "by reason and will" *(intellectu et voluntate),* not physical forces that act "by natural necessity" *(de necessitate naturae).* Only for the intelligences does the possibility exist of causing motion that takes place in the absence of resistance and yet is still of finite velocity.

This is the reason why Buridan's attempt to replace the intelligences by impetus must have seemed somewhat bold, even from the standpoint of a natural philosopher. No impetus, not even a celestial impetus, can be a detached mover *(motor separatus)* of the exceptional type just mentioned; impetus is a normal, mechanical force that must obey the general laws. Buridan does not touch on this difficulty himself, but Oresme saw it and tried to modify Buridan's theory in this respect as well. One of his early questions on the *De sphaera* is of interest in this regard. It is, in fact, the same question as the one we quoted earlier, and it reads as follows: "Is this a true conditional: if the mover of the heavens were in magnitude, it would move instantaneously." Oresme's answer, which we may assume is directed against Buridan's hypothesis, is summarized in five *conclusiones.*

> The first conclusion is that in the heavens there is no resistance by which a mover might be impeded. The second conclusion is that every natural force that is like a quality can produce mo-

tion in the presence of some resistance. The third conclusion is that if any natural force should be applied to a passive object which offers no resistance, then the force would move it instantaneously. The fourth conclusion is that every force that is inherently in magnitude is a natural force, not a volitional one. The final conclusion is that if the force moving the heavens is in magnitude, then it is not a volitional force but a natural one, as the fourth conclusion demonstrates; and if this were so, then it would be possible to move the heavens instantaneously without resistance as the third conclusion shows, since the heavens would offer no resistance, as we know from the first conclusion.[23]

Oresme later changed his mind. In his late *Traité du ciel et du monde,* which appeared in 1377, he follows Buridan in asserting that the heavens are moved by mechanical forces, but he does not regard them as analogues to terrestrial forces, considering them instead in a general way as inherent motive qualities. This supposition requires him to assume that there is resistance to celestial motion too. The attempt to define this motion further leads him to conjecture that the resistance that the heavens oppose to the forces moving them consists in a tendency to preserve their characteristic velocity: "For the resistance that is in the heavens does not tend to some other motion or to rest, but only to not being moved any faster."[24]

23. Vat. lat. 2185, fol. 75r–v (qu. 9). The propositions are given without the proofs (except for the last conclusion). ["Prima conclusio, quod in ipso caelo non est aliqua resistentia per quam resistat motori.—Secunda conclusio, quod omnis virtus naturalis, quae est sicut qualitas, potest movere cum aliqua resistentia.—Tertia conclusio, quod si aliqua virtus naturalis applicetur passo habenti resistentiam, ipsa moveret illud in instanti.—Quarta conclusio, quod omnis virtus, quae est in magnitudine inhaerente, est virtus naturalis et non voluntaria.—Ultima conclusio, quod si virtus movens caelum esset in magnitudine, tunc moveret caelum in instanti. Probatur: quia si esset in magnitudine, esset virtus non voluntaria, sed naturalis per quartam conclusionem; et si ita esset, tunc posset movere caelum sine resistentia in instanti per tertiam conclusionem, quia caelum nullam habet resistentiam per primam conclusionem."]

24. *Traité,* livre II, chap. 3. [Menut and Denomy, 1968, p. 298. "Car la resistance qui est au ciel ne l'encline pas a autre mouvement ne a repos, mais seulement a ce que il ne soit meu plus ysnellement."]

Now, in formulating this position Oresme in fact enunciates the essential feature of what is later called the law of inertia: an object in uniform motion tends to preserve its velocity—it tends neither toward some other motion nor toward a state of rest—and it offers resistance to any attempt to accelerate it. But this principle still applies only to celestial mechanics and not to terrestrial conditions. Moreover, we have already seen that Oresme formulated his concept of impetus entirely analogously to Newton's concept of force, as a cause of acceleration, not of constant velocity. However, this principle applies only to terrestrial mechanics, not to celestial motions. If Oresme had combined these two hypotheses, which are really only two components of the same idea, then we would be fully justified in regarding him as the first thinker to discover the law of inertia. But that is precisely what he did not do. Furthermore, because his version of impetus attracted almost no attention and did not undergo any further development, no one else ever thought his discovery through to its logical conclusion.

As mentioned, Buridan does not address the question of whether an impetus would move the heavens like a detached mover *(motor separatus)* in the absence of resistance or whether it is necessary to assume that there is a certain kind of resistance specially designed to balance off the impetus without destroying it. All he provides is a sketchy hypothesis rather than a fully developed theory. Here, again, Buridan neglected to follow up a position, even though he had expressed himself unequivocally on the matter in another context. It is by no means obvious that the absence of all resistance is a sufficient condition for the infinite duration of celestial motion.

There is, finally, one other question that sheds some light on the nature of scholastic impetus, although from an entirely different perspective. If it were true that an impetus acting in the realm of terrestrial events and in the absence of resistance could produce motion of finite velocity, would this motion last forever? Scholastic philosophers never explicitly posed this question, but they in fact answered it. One question they did ask was, What causes a particular motion to last as long as it does; on what factors does the greater or lesser duration of a motion depend? This was a problem in its own right, independent both of the laws of motion governing the relationship between force, resistance, and velocity and of the theory of projectile motion. It was usually discussed in the context of the widespread debate about whether the infinite duration of celestial motion[25] implies that the first mover is infinite in intensity and whether Aristotle intended to draw this conclusion. The question was normally discussed at the beginning of the eighth book of the *Physics*, but it was also the subject of numerous special inquiries. To put it another way, they asked, Does uniform motion of infinite duration in a resistanceless environment presuppose a force of infinite magnitude, or would a finite force suffice? This is the converse of the question posed at the beginning of the paragraph: Would a (finite) impetus continue to operate forever under the stipulated (albeit impossible) conditions?

The problem provoked considerable discussion and attracted a variety of different solutions. There was unanimous agreement on only a single assumption, and it usually provided the starting point for the debate. Indeed, so universal was its acceptance that no other idea had the slightest chance of being taken into consideration. The assumption was a rule specifying that, in the normal functioning of the laws of nature, a motion of greater duration requires "more" force or "more" power than one of lesser duration, all other things being equal. For instance, "to move for two days takes more force than to move for only one." From this proposition it of course follows that an infinite amount of force is necessary to produce a motion of infinite duration. What the problem ultimately reduces to is, In what sense is the infinity of force or power mentioned here to be understood?

However, the rule itself deserves closer examination, since once it has been conceded, the question has really been answered. The kind of motion it is applied to here is celestial motion, that is, constant velocity motion occurring in the absence of resistance, which is, of course, the scholastic analogue to inertial motion. And according to the rule, such motion has the property that more force or power is required to move the same object under the same conditions for two days instead of one. But whatever operates in this fashion when there is "more" of it is obviously something different

25. Which for Aristotle was a fact and for Christian philosophers was possible (at least in the future).

from that factor in the causal structure of motion whose alterations bring about changes in the intensity of velocity given constant resistance. To put it briefly (since I have already treated the whole topic in more detail elsewhere),[26] the power or force that determines the duration of motion, all other things being equal, was viewed by the fourteenth-century natural philosophers in the last analysis as nothing other than a kind of energy reserve that transforms itself into motion and that naturally lasts longer if there is "more" of it. Every motion uses energy in this sense, even celestial motion. (Of course, it should be remembered that these concepts must be taken with a grain of salt.) And the eternal duration of celestial motion is in fact attributed to a certain infiniteness associated with it, only what is meant here is not infinite intensity but rather a sort of inexhaustibility or *infatigabilitas* that corresponds to an infinite amount of energy.[27]

Thus in scholastic theory there are motive forces, the so-called *vires infatigabiles* or *intransmutabiles,* which differ from normal terrestrial forces in that they can cause motion for any length of time without being used up. They are the only forces to which the rule does not apply that a motion that lasts longer requires "more" force than a shorter one, since, as Walter Burley puts it, "in the case of an inexhaustible mover no more force is required to produce motion for two days instead of one, nor is more force required to produce motion for eight days instead of one, and so on

26. "Das Lehrstück von den 'vires infatigabiles' in der scholastischen Naturphilosophie," *Archives internationales d'histoire des sciences* 5 (1952): 6–44; and *Metaphysische Hintergründe,* chap. IV.

27. A word should be said about the terminology here in order to avoid possible misunderstandings. The *infatigabilitas* that is referred to in the commentaries on Book VIII of Aristotle's *Physics* (and in the related questions) is not the direct opposite of the *fatigatio* that is considered in the questions on *De caelo* mentioned above (footnotes 17–20). In the latter case it is (following the usual distinction made by fourteenth-century philosophers) a *fatigatio in operando* (or *in ordine ad effectum*), whereas in the former it is an *infatigabilitas* (or *perpetuitas*) *in essendo* that is not only guaranteed like the other by the lack of resistance but that also represents a special ontological factor.

to infinity."[28] Buridan explains that "a force no matter how small suffices to produce motion forever as long as it is *intransmutabilis*, because such a force can by definition produce motion for one hour and by the same definition for all time."[29] The only forces besides the first mover itself that have this special feature are those forces that operate to some degree "as organs and as instruments" of the first mover and draw directly on the infinite source of energy that the first mover represents. They are the powers that move the heavens, whether considered in the traditional fashion to be intelligences, that is, detached movers *(motores separati)*, or, as Buridan would have it, to be impetuses that God himself transmitted to the spheres at the moment of creation. In both cases it is the relationship to the first mover that guarantees the inexhaustibility *(infatigabilitas)* of the forces.

Conversely, a temporal impetus could only produce motion of unlimited duration if it were likewise an inexhaustible force, that is, either an infinite source of energy itself or the "organ and instrument" of such a source. But of course this is not the case. An impetus caused by a human being is just as finite and limited as the motive force from which it derives. The same rule therefore applies to it that applies to all forces capable of being changed and destroyed. The longer the motion lasts, the greater (in the sense of amount of energy) the motive force must be; conversely, motion only lasts until the available reserve of energy is used up or, in this case, until the impetus transmitted to the projectile is used up.

This aspect of the definition of impetus perhaps provides the real key to its understanding. Impetus is not so much a force for which there is no analogue in classical mechanics as it is a special

28. Burley, *Physica* VIII, tract. 4 (Venice, 1482 and 1491). ["Non maior virtus requiritur in motore infatigabili ad movendum per duos dies quam per unum diem, nec requiritur maior virtus ad movendum per octo dies quam per unum diem, et sic multiplicando in infinitum."]

29. Buridan, *Physica* VIII, qu. 9. He also makes a similar statement in *Metaphysica* XII, qu. 6. ["Quia sufficit ad movendum perpetuo tempore virtus quantumcumque parva, dum tamen ipsa sit intransmutabilis, quia talis qua ratione potest movere per unam horam, et eadem ratione per omne tempus."]

kind of energy that has no counterpart in modern physics and whose nature it is to be transformed into motion.[30] Moreover, this energy is *always* depleted, even in the case of uniform motion. Viewed from this standpoint, impetus embodies a fundamentally different attitude from that which finds expression in the law of inertia.

30. Seventeenth-century thinkers probably still thought of energy in a similar fashion. Gassendi and his followers (who included in this regard not only true atomists but the likes of Leibniz and Newton, that is, all those who did not want to join Descartes in rejecting the notion of primary forces) postulated the existence of certain innate motive forces in the ultimate particles that are supposed to give rise to corpuscular motions. These latter motions were regarded as the basis of all earthly change. Gassendi considered the primary atomic force (or, more correctly, atomic energy) to be nothing other "than the natural and internal capacity or power which enables the atom to stir or move itself; or, if you will, an inborn, innate, native, and undying tendency and drive and *impetus* from within." And the reason, according to him, why Epicurus went beyond Democritus and introduced this power that gives rise to atomic motion and refused to be satisfied with the idea of primary motions is this: "He thought it absurd not to attribute a special power to [the atoms] by which such motion might be produced; gravity or weight, or impulsion and *impetus* are [powers] of this kind, and it is true that whatever is acted upon by them is moved." (For more on these passages and this idea see *Die Mechanisierung des Weltbildes im 17. Jahrhundert* [Leipzig: F. Meiner, 1938], p. 19 f.) [Now reprinted in *Zwei Untersuchungen zur nachscholastischen Philosophie,* 2d ed. (Rome: Edizioni di Storia e Letteratura, 1968).] This innate motive force in the atoms is clearly nothing other than a scholastic impetus, specifically an inexhaustible impetus as employed by Buridan to explain the motion of the heavens. (The difference is that Buridan's impetus causes circular motion; Gassendi's, rectilinear.) It is a potency that stands somewhere between force and energy and sustains motion in the absence of resistance; it is indestructible and inexhaustible, and by its very nature it transforms itself perpetually into uniform motion. From the perspective of classical physics, of course, such a concept is superfluous. Nevertheless, the eminent founders of the new physics continued, with few exceptions, to employ it when, *as philosophers,* they sought to account for the workings of the microcosm (if I may use this term), and they limited the application of the law of inertia to the mechanics of the macrocosm.

Five:

GALILEO AND
THE SCHOLASTIC THEORY
OF IMPETUS

In the preceding chapter Maier argued that the theory of impetus, considered in the context of scholastic mechanics, cannot be regarded as an anticipation of the law of inertia. This does not mean, however, that it did not play a role in the process by which the concept of inertial motion was discovered. By 1600 it had become a standard element of physical theory, and it continued to influence natural philosophers throughout the seventeenth century, particularly in their explanations of acceleration during free fall. Even nonscholastic thinkers who rejected impetus in favor of rival theories were necessarily acquainted with its principles and applications.

To illustrate the importance of the theory of impetus in the transition from scholastic to nonscholastic mechanics in the seventeenth century, Maier focuses on the writings of Galileo Galilei (d. 1642), the first representative of modern mechanics and experimental physics. Considerable research has been devoted to the problem of the relationship between Galileo's thought and that of his medieval predecessors, but as yet no general solution has emerged. This much is certain: in his early years, when he was a professor of mathematics first at Pisa and then at Padua (1589–1610), Galileo was an outspoken advocate of the concept of impetus or impressed force, although his views concerning its nature changed during this time. In the following essay Maier analyzes the version of the theory of impetus advanced by Galileo in his early unpub-

lished treatise on motion, De motu *(ca. 1590) and shows how it differs from the standard scholastic treatment of impetus and conflicts with the modern concept of inertia. She then turns to his mature defense of Copernicus's heliocentric model of the solar system, the* Dialogue on the Two Chief World Systems *(1632), and shows that Galileo had by this time implicitly, if not explicitly, abandoned the basic outlook of scholastic mechanics and adopted a position logically equivalent to the law of inertia. In making this transition, Maier concludes, Galileo achieved the breakthrough that had eluded fourteenth-century scholastic thinkers, but he did so initially within the framework of the theory of impetus.*

The essay translated here, "Galilei und die scholastische Impetustheorie," is one of Anneliese Maier's last essays on the subject of natural philosophy. It appeared both in Saggi su Galileo Galilei *(Florence: G. Barberà, 1972), and in* Ausgehendes Mittelalter, *vol. 2 (Rome: Edizioni di Storia e Letteratura, 1967), pp. 465–90. This translation is based on the latter text. I have omitted Maier's introductory discussion on the nature and history of the concept of impetus (pp. 469–76), since this material is covered in the preceding selection. Because of these omissions and because the Latin wording of the passages cited in the text is included in the footnotes, the numbering of the footnotes is entirely new.*

The works of the young Galileo and the writings of his Pisan period reveal a man who was to a surprising extent a disciple of late scholastic natural philosophy. Late scholasticism was in essence an elaboration of Aristotelian cosmology that reached its highest stage of development at Paris and Oxford in the fourteenth century and then served as the traditional body of scientific knowledge for the succeeding two centuries. In Galileo's early works one finds most of the topics that scholastic thinkers commonly discussed, including the problems of *intensio et remissio formarum, mixtio* of the elements, *maxima et minima,* and *actio et reactio.* Only one of these questions, however, played a substantial and perhaps decisive role in Galileo's development, namely, the scholastic theory of impetus. . . .

By the end of the sixteenth century, the theory of impetus was universally known and accepted by every school of thought, although no significant modifications had been made to the theory since it was first developed in the fourteenth century. Galileo was apparently unacquainted with Buridan's commentary on the *Physics,* in which the classic presentation of the theory is found; at least he never cited the work, which was available in a printed edition from 1509. It is even less likely that Galileo knew anything of Nicole Oresme, whose commentaries on the *Physics* and *De caelo* had never been published. Nor does he mention Albert of Saxony, although he does refer to Marsilius of Inghen, but only in regard to other topics. Yet Galileo had many other opportunities to become acquainted with impetus theory, and like most of his contemporaries he presumably had learned the substance of the theory at second or third hand. It is often said of Galileo that he read little of other authors and hardly ever referred to them, but this is only true of his later years. In his youth he knew the contemporary literature well or at least knew what positions many authors had taken on particular questions. In his early writings Galileo cites numerous authorities for every problem except one: in the chapter on impetus he refers to no other work. This is highly significant, since it shows that for Galileo, as for many of his contemporaries, impetus theory had become a completely obvious doctrine, one that was so well known and evident that no one felt obliged to adduce authorities to justify it. . . .

Considerable discussion has been devoted to the problem of determining which seventeenth-century thinker was the "real" discoverer of the law of inertia and whether Galileo deserves the credit for having stated it, at least in an implicit form. The answer depends on how one defines the "discovery" of the law of inertia, and on this point opinions differ widely. From the standpoint of the physicist, the discoverer can only be the person who first correctly formulated the concept of the preservation of uniform motion in the language of mathematical physics.[1] On the other hand, if one approaches the problem from the standpoint of medieval natural philosophy, the

---

1. R. J. Seeger, "On the Role of Galileo in Physics" in *Physis* 5 (1963):5–38, provides an example of this approach, but it is an example of how *not* to do it. The essay displays a lack of understanding of the conceptual world of the Middle Ages (and of those who concern themselves with it) that is hard to exaggerate, and, correspondingly, it fails to comprehend the historical background and the development of ideas that led to the new physics.

question is to determine when, by whom, and in what context the fundamental and revolutionary idea first arose that terrestrial motion initiated by a human being continues independent of him and can last forever if unaffected by outside forces. The crucial point is that the first suggestion of such an idea represented the beginning of a new era, since the whole concept would have been shocking and utterly absurd both for Aristotelianism and the whole of scholasticism—even for late scholasticism despite the other discoveries it had made about nature. It is therefore unessential whether this discovery was applied from the start to linear rather than circular motion and even less important how this new law of inertia was formulated quantitatively. Before the discovery was stated in physical terms there first had to be a metaphysical-ontological breakthrough, a change to some degree in world view, that is, a modification of conceptions concerning motion, the forces that cause motion, and, above all, the inertia of moving bodies. This new realization that the fundamental axioms of scholastic mechanics were incorrect and had to be replaced can justifiably be regarded as the initial discovery of the law of inertia, since the new axioms prepared the way for the later physical and mathematical formulation of the law itself.

In this essay I propose to show that this essential transformation was accomplished by Galileo years before Descartes formulated his law of conservation or Isaac Beeckman wrote his *Journal,* and, furthermore, that Galileo did so within the framework of scholastic impetus theory, which he adhered to all his life but modified in decisive ways, perhaps without being fully aware that he had done so. . . .

Among the fragments of the [early] treatise *De motu*[2] there is a chapter devoted to the question "What moves projectiles" *(a quo moveatur proiecta)?* In his answer Galileo adopts the scholastic theory of impetus without hesitation. He deviates from the traditional

2. *Le Opere di Galileo Galilei,* Edizione nazionale, 20 vols. (Florence: G. Barberà, 1890–1909), 1: 251–419. [Also available in: Galileo Galilei, *On Motion and On Mechanics,* comprising *De Motu* (ca. 1590), trans. I. E. Drabkin, and *Le Meccaniche* (ca. 1600), trans. Stillman Drake (Madison, Wis.: University of Wisconsin Press, 1960).]

explanation in a few details, but on all essential points he accepts it and makes it his own. The main outlines of his argument are as follows.

Galileo begins with an observation that fourteenth-century philosophers used to make in a similar fashion: "As in almost everything he wrote about local motion, Aristotle wrote the opposite of the truth on this question as well."[3] In this particular case the source of the error is the Aristotelian axiom that every motion requires a mover in contact with the moving object, since it forces Aristotle to postulate that a projectile is propelled forward by the surrounding air after it leaves the thrower's hand. So far Galileo is unquestionably right. But in the next part of his discussion of Aristotle's theory he falls into error himself:

> Aristotle therefore supposes that the mover, for example the thrower of a stone, also drives the adjacent parts of air before he releases the stone, and they, he says, likewise move other parts, and these still other parts, and so forth in successive stages; and the stone, once it leaves the thrower, is then carried by these parts of air, whence arises a certain discontinuous motion of the stone, so that it is not one motion but many.[4]

According to Galileo, Aristotle taught that the original mover sets both the projectile and the surrounding air into motion at the same time and that the first "wave" of air moves the next "wave" adjoining it, which then moves another one further on, and so forth. These successive "waves" of air are supposed to carry the projectile along with them. Earlier commentators had also occasionally misunderstood Aristotle's theory in this or some similar way. Aristotle's actual explanation of detached motion *(motus separatus)* is different. The mover imparts to the air not only a *moveri* but also a *movere*; that is, he not only moves the air (along with the projectile in his

3. ["Aristoteles, sicut fere in omnibus quae de motu locali scripsit, in hac etiam quaestione vero contrarium scripsit."]

4. ["Vult igitur Aristoteles motorem, ut v.gr. proicientem lapidem, priusquam lapidem relinquat, pellere etiam partes aeris contiguas, quas, inquit, similiter movere alias partes, has alias, et sic successive; lapidem autem a proiciente relictum deinde ferri a partibus illius aeris et sic fieri motum quendam lapidis discontinuum, et non esse unicum motum sed plures."]

hand), but he also transfers to it a portion of his motive force. This is possible because the two media of air and water have, among other special properties, an ability to take on such motive forces. In this they differ from solid bodies, which cannot receive such transfers of motive force. Thus first the "wave" of air adjacent to the projectile and the hand of the mover receives a motive force that operates in the direction determined by the thrower. This force then imparts a similar but weaker motive force to the neighboring "wave" of air, and so forth, in such a fashion that the force decreases at every stage until none is left. It is these forces, not the "waves" of air themselves, that, in Aristotle's view, move the projectile onward.

Galileo notes immediately after the sentence just quoted that "this attempt is an evasion by Aristotle and his followers, who were not able to understand how an object can be moved by an impressed force or what kind of force this is."[5] But such criticism is not entirely justified. Aristotle, as we have just seen, was thoroughly convinced that a projectile is moved by an impressed force, although he thought it was imparted to the medium. Long before it was developed into a real doctrine in the impetus theory of the fourteenth century, this idea that a moving body can take on an imparted force *(vis derelicta)* had already appeared here and there in the works of earlier commentators. Johannes Philoponus (or Grammaticus) was probably the first thinker to analyze the idea in detail, but his commentary on the *Physics* that contains the discussion was unknown in the Middle Ages. The work was first translated into Latin in the sixteenth century. Galileo was acquainted with a translation printed in 1535 that he cites repeatedly, although not in connection with the theory of impetus. Nevertheless, it is possible that this commentary was one of the sources from which he derived his knowledge of impressed force.

Galileo first refutes the Aristotelian theory and then explains impetus theory and illustrates it with examples: "So that the other

5. ["Huc conatus est aufugere Aristoteles et eius sectatores qui sibi persuadere non potuerunt, quomodo posset mobile a virtute impressa moveri, aut quid ista esset virtus."]

opinion may be known to be correct, we will first try to destroy completely the one of Aristotle; [then] we will explain the other, that is the one about impressed force, until it is clear and illustrate it with examples."[6]

The objections that he raises against Aristotle are, with one exception to be discussed shortly, no different from those that Franciscus de Marchia and Buridan first employed and that others had raised repeatedly ever since. If the medium moves the projectile onward after it separates from the original mover, how can an arrow fly against a strong wind? Or, how can a ship that is being towed against the current continue to move forward for a time after it is released? In the first case it is unthinkable that the air moved by a man's hand can possess greater force than a strong wind. Furthermore, if the moving medium carries the projectile with it, what makes an iron ball fly farther, all other things being equal, than an equally large wooden ball or a bit of straw? These are some of the classic objections. Another, especially noteworthy objection will be considered further on.

Galileo concludes:

> We believe that these are arguments which more than suffice to refute that absurd opinion, which those who are not able to understand what an impressed force is try to maintain. Now, however, in order to explain our opinion, let us first ask what that motive force is, which is impressed by a thrower on a projectile.[7]

Galileo thus raises a question also posed by fourteenth-century thinkers, "What sort of thing is impetus?" *(qualis res est ille impetus)*, for which no completely clear and generally accepted answer had ever been found. Everybody agreed, in any case, that the impressed

6. ["Verum, ut altera opinio verissima innotescat, hanc prius Aristotelis funditus evertere conabimur; alteram vero de virtute impressa, quoad licuerit, declarabimus et exemplis illustrabimus."]

7. ["Hae sint rationes quibus satis superque confutare credimus ineptam illam sententiam quem, qui sibi suadere non possunt quid sit illa virtus impressa, tueri conatur. Nunc autem, ut sententiam nostram explicemus, inquiramus primo, quid sit ista virtus motive, quae a proiciente in proiecto imprimitur."]

force is a quality in the Aristotelian sense. But opinions began to diverge as soon as the next questions were asked: to which of the four subspecies of quality does it belong, and what is its categorical relationship to the other motive forces?

Galileo solves this problem with a hypothesis of his own that is rather unusual from the standpoint both of impetus theory and of modern physics. "We say, therefore, that it is the privation of gravity when the object is thrown upward and the privation of levity when it is thrown downward."[8] Thus, when the object is thrown straight up in the air, the impetus given to it is a "removal of heaviness"; when it is thrown straight downward, the impetus is a "removal of lightness." Galileo does not consider horizontal and oblique trajectories at all, although they constitute by far the majority of cases. Basically, Galileo did not intend so much to give an ontological definition of impetus with this explanation, which explains nothing, as to prepare the way for his theory of acceleration during free fall, which he presents in his next chapter.

This renowned theory, which he continued to advocate in the *Dialogue on the Two Chief World Systems* and the *Discourses Concerning Two New Sciences*, holds that when a body is projected upward violently it receives an upwardly directed impressed force that at first is stronger than the body's natural heaviness *(gravitas)*. Gradually, however, the impressed force decreases (for reasons to be considered shortly) until the two forces reach a state of equilibrium. This is the turning point. From this moment on the heaviness predominates and the body begins to fall. But it does not immediately fall with that full velocity corresponding to its heaviness that Galileo, like the scholastics, regarded as a constant quantity. Instead, the body's downward movement is hindered initially by the impetus that still remains, since at the turning point the impetus is not destroyed but only reduced to equality with the body's heaviness. The impetus continues to exist for the duration of the fall and constitutes a continually decreasing counterforce to the body's

8. ["Dicimus ergo illam esse privationem gravitatis, cum mobile sursum pellitur, cum vero deorsum, esse privationem levitatis."]

gravity. Thus the motion of a body in free fall is retarded at first, but the resistance becomes progressively weaker until the impetus is exhausted and the moving body finally reaches its characteristic, constant velocity.[9] Galileo emphasizes that in practice this latter condition is usually not achieved because the distance through which the body falls is too short.[10] In any case, however, he rejects Aristotle's explanation, since it specifies that the velocity of a falling body would become infinite if the center of the world, toward which the body moves and which coincides *per accidens* with the earth's center, were moved infinitely far away. Galileo's idea still applies even if no violent upward motion immediately precedes the free fall, for if a body is in a raised position, some kind of forcible raising must have taken place earlier. The body preserves the impetus it received when it was thrown upward or raised to a higher position if it is prevented from falling by some external impediment such as a supporting surface. The impetus in this situation is exactly equal to the body's gravity, and it begins to act the moment the impediment is removed and the body starts to fall.

This idea differs greatly from classic impetus theory. For scholastic thinkers it would have been inconceivable that an impressed force could be conserved after the body had come to rest. In their view this was a clear example of the difference between natural and violent motive forces. Gravity is an inexhaustible force *(vis infatigabilis)* whose operation can be temporarily hindered but never destroyed; thus it is unquestionably capable of this sort of conservation. Impetus, on the other hand, is an exhaustible and corruptible force *(vis fatigabilis et corruptibilis)* that is destroyed as soon as some form of resistance overcomes it. Therefore, arrival at a state of rest, or the turning point of an uninterrupted motion,

---

9. The scholastic conception of this process is just the opposite: the "real" (constant) speed of descent that corresponds to the body's weight is the initial speed, which is increased by the additional impetus acquired during the descent.

10. This can at best only happen in the case of very light bodies, since, according to Galileo, experience shows that they reach their nominal velocity relatively quickly.

signifies that the impetus imparted to the body has been annihilated and that from this moment on only its gravity continues to operate.

Galileo makes no attempt to develop in detail or elucidate his definition of impressed force. Instead, he proceeds immediately to the next question: How can a removal of heaviness *(privatio gravitatis)* or, as he also puts it, a (violently produced) lightness *(levitas)* be imparted by the thrower to the projectile? To answer this question he gives some analogous cases of qualitative change that consist of examples deriving wholly from the conceptual world of scholasticism and that were in common use long before his time. They originated in attempts to prove that an impressed force can be transferred not only to media, as Aristotle said, but to solid bodies as well. The first analogy is as follows: "But anyone who is not surprised that fire is able to remove coldness from iron by introducing heat will not be surprised that a thrower, by sending a heavy object upward, can remove its heaviness and give it lightness." He then continues:

> But here is another, more beautiful example. You wonder what leaves the hand of the thrower and is impressed on the projectile; but do you not wonder what leaves the hammer and is transferred to the bell of a clock, and how so much sound can be given to a silent bell by a silent hammer, and how it is maintained in the bell once the hammer stops striking?[11]

The process by which the thrower imparts to the projectile a motive quality *(qualitas motiva)* that counteracts its natural gravity is compared to the way in which the natural coldness of iron is suppressed (but not destroyed) when it is forcibly heated and to the action through which a bell, although by nature silent, is made to ring

11. ["Quomodo autem proiciens possit, sursum dirigendo grave, ipsum gravitate privare et leve reddere, non mirabitur is qui non miratur quomodo ignis possit privare ferrum frigiditate, introducendo calorem." And: "Sed esto aliud pulcrius exemplum. Miraris quid ex manu proicientis exeat et in proiectum imprimatur; et non miraris quid e malleo exeat et in horologii campanam transferatur et unde tantus sonus e silente malleo in silentem campanam traducatur, et quomodo in ea, absente qui percussit, conservetur."]

when its natural stillness is suppressed by a sonorous quality
(qualitas sonora).

Galileo examines each of these examples in greater detail:

> Therefore a projectile is moved upward by the thrower when it
> is in his hand, and it is deprived of heaviness; the iron is likewise
> moved by an alterative motion toward heat when it is in the fire,
> and it is deprived of coldness by the fire. The motive force, that
> is the lightness, is preserved in the stone after the thrower stops
> holding it; the heat is preserved in the iron when it is removed
> from the fire. The impressed force in the projectile decreases
> gradually once the thrower is gone; the heat in the iron decreases
> once the fire is gone. The stone is finally brought to rest; the iron
> likewise returns to its natural coldness.[12]

He continues:

> The bell is struck by the striker; the stone is moved by the mover.
> The bell is deprived of silence; the stone is deprived of rest. A
> sonorous quality contrary to its natural silence is introduced into
> the bell; a motive quality contrary to its rest is introduced into
> the stone. The sound is preserved in the bell once the striker is
> gone; the motion is preserved in the stone once the mover is gone.
> The sonorous quality in the bell decreases gradually; the motive
> quality in the stone decreases gradually.[13]

The impressed force gradually decreases, just as the forcibly
heated iron slowly cools and the sound of the bell fades away and

12. ["Movetur igitur sursum mobile a proiciente, dum in manu illius est,
et gravitate privatur; movetur similiter motu alterativo ferrum ad calorem,
dum ferrum est in igne, et ab eo privatur frigiditate. Virtus motiva, nempe
levitas, conservatur in lapide, non tangente qui movit; calor conservatur in
ferro ab igne remoto. Virtus impressa successive remittitur in proiecto,
proiciente absente; calor remittitur in ferro, igne absente. Lapis tandem
reducitur ad quietem; ferrum similiter ad naturalem frigiditatem redit."]

13. ["Pulsatur a pulsante campana; movetur a movente lapis. Privatur
campana silentio; privatur lapis quiete. Introducitur in campanam qualitas
sonora contraria eius naturali silentio; introducitur in lapidem qualitas
motiva contraria illius quieti. Conservatur in campana sonus, absente qui
pulsavit; conservatur in lapide motus, absente qui movit. Remittitur successive in campana qualitas sonora; gradatim remittitur in lapide qualitas
motiva."]

finally dies out. This phenomenon of gradual decrease (*gradatim remitti*) happens by itself and does not involve destruction by opposing qualities. Galileo repeatedly calls attention to the idea in the succeeding chapters, as in this example: "It must be noted that the contrary quality in a moving object does not decrease because it is opposed by the heaviness of the body; . . . instead, the quality becomes weaker by itself and leaves the moving object."[14]

In assuming that heaviness has no destructive effect whatsoever on impressed force, Galileo again deviates from the traditional teaching. But his notion that impetus becomes weaker and dies out by itself, regardless of all external influences, is in full accord with a key point of scholastic theory. This gradual self-consumption and ultimate extinction, this natural transience, was a characteristic feature of impetus.

Galileo devotes another short chapter to the problem of the diminution of impressed force. He ends the detailed discussion of the causes of projectile motion as follows:

> Therefore let us finally conclude that projectiles are in no way moved by the medium, but rather by a force impressed by the thrower. Now, however, let us proceed to demonstrate that this force gradually decreases, and that in a violent motion no two points can be specified at which the motive force is the same.

A short chapter follows, entitled: "In which it is shown that the motive force in a moving object gradually becomes weaker."[15]

Galileo begins by showing that since projectiles are moved by impressed force, it immediately follows that violent motion is not composed of several separate motions as Aristotle maintained, but is undivided and continuous. He then continues:

14. *Opere,* Edizione nazionale 1:335. ["Est animadvertendum in mobili qualitatem illam contrariam non ideo remitti, quia a gravitate eiusdem mobilis oppugnetur, . . . sed qualitas illa per se debilitatur et mobile relinquit."]

15. ["Concludamus igitur tandem proiecta nullo modo moveri a medio, sed a virtute impressa a proiciente. Nunc autem prosequamur ostendere hanc virtutem successive diminui nec posse in motu violento duo puncta assignari, in quibus eadem fuerit virtus motiva." The title: "In quo virtutem motivam successive in mobili debilitari ostenditur."]

Because this is so, and violent motion is not infinite, it follows necessarily that the force impressed by the thrower decreases continually in the projectile, and no two points of time in that motion can be given at which the motive power is the same and not weaker.[16]

He thus infers from the fact that a violent motion cannot be of infinite duration ("nothing violent is eternal" was a basic principle of Aristotelian and scholastic metaphysics) that the force that the thrower imparts to the body and that causes its motion must become progressively weaker. To "prove" this assertion he first of all assumes that "the same object is moved by the same force, in the same medium and on the same line, with the same velocity."[17] In other words, all other things being equal, the speed of the moving body depends on the strength of its impetus; if its impetus is equally strong at two points in the trajectory, then the body's speed must be the same at these two points. But, the argument continues, if it is possible to find two points *(c* and *d)* at which the impressed force is the same, then the impressed force is necessarily the same at *all* points, since there is no reason why it should change between points *c* and *d* or between *d* and any other point equally far away as *c*. This would mean, however, that the violent motion would never weaken, but rather last forever and go on to infinity with the same motive force and the same velocity. To accept such a conclusion would be the height of absurdity:

Hence, if the same argument is repeated, it will be demonstrated that the violent motion never decreases, but carries on with the same velocity forever and to infinity, always having the same motive force; and this is certainly most absurd.[18]

16. ["Quod cum ita sit nec motus violentus infinitus sit, sequitur necessario virtutem illam a proiciente impressam continue in proiecto remitti, nec posse dari in eo motu duo puncta temporis in quibus eadem virtus motiva sit et non debilior."]

17. ["Idem mobile ab eadem virtute in eodem medio et super eandem lineam eadem cum velocitate moveri."]

18. ["Quare, eadem argumentatione repetita demonstrabitur, motum violentum nunquam remitti, sed eadem velocitate semper et in infinitum ferri, eadem semper manente virtute motiva: quod certe absurdissimum est."]

Galileo thus "proves" in this chapter a proposition that is the exact opposite of the law of inertia; or, to put it more precisely, he deduces a proposition that is the exact analogue of the law of inertia expressed in the language of impetus theory, and he declares it, and consequently the assumptions it is based on, to be absurd. He concludes: "Therefore it is not true that two points of a violent motion can be specified at which the driving force remains the same; and this was to be demonstrated."[19] This proof could have been presented in exactly the same way by a fourteenth-century thinker.

In the preceding chapter of Galileo's treatise (that was summarized earlier) there is a statement that indicates how remote Galileo's thinking was at this time from the idea that a motion and its cause can last forever. In the earlier discussion I passed over one of Galileo's arguments against the Aristotelian theory of projectile motion that is of particular interest. Galileo wishes to show that Aristotle contradicted himself in the process of presenting the notion that moving air is the mover of a detached projectile:

> Aristotle does not seem to be really sure of himself. For in 3rd *Caelo* text 27 he says: if something that is moved is neither heavy nor light, it will be moved violently; and whatever is moved violently and possesses no resistance in the form of heaviness or lightness moves forever. In the following text, however, he says that projectiles are carried by the medium. Therefore, since air has neither heaviness nor lightness, the motion caused in it by a thrower will go on forever and always at the same velocity. And thus it will carry projectiles forever and will not wear out, since it is always moved by the same force. But experience teaches us the opposite of this.[20]

19. ["Non ergo verum est, in motu violento posse duo puncta assignari, in quibus eadem maneat virtus impellans; quod demonstrandum fuit."]

20. ["Non bene sibi constare videtur Aristoteles. Nam 3° Caeli text. 27 inquit: si quod movetur neque grave neque leve fuerit, vi movebitur; et quod vi movetur nullam gravitatis aut levitatis resistentiam habens, in infinitum movetur. Textu autem sequenti inquit proiecta a medio ferri:

This critique relies on the same kind of argument we encountered earlier. A passage from Aristotle is interpreted to mean that the motion that the thrower imparts to the air and that is then supposed to carry the projectile onward could persist unchanged for all eternity. This conclusion, however, is rejected as absurd.

Galileo recapitulates Aristotle's theory so as to imply that Aristotle advanced a proposition that corresponds to the law of inertia: "Whatever is moved violently and possesses no resistance in the form of heaviness or lightness, moves forever." A projectile moving in the absence of resistance, then, will continue to move forever. In reality, Aristotle did not say this. What we have here is a characteristic misunderstanding on Galileo's part. In the passage that Galileo cites, Aristotle wants to show that the idea that bodies without heaviness or lightness could exist leads to absurd consequences and is itself therefore absurd. If such a body were moved violently, then an infinite motion *(motus infinitus)*, not a motion lasting forever *(motus in infinitum)*, would result, since no resistance would be present. The moving body would be able to cover any given interval in an infinitely short span of time. For Aristotle, the total absence of resistance always entails the same result: infinite velocity, but not a motion of infinite duration. All the scholastic philosophers who discussed this passage in their commentaries understood it correctly, and it really should not be misunderstood, since Aristotle specified exactly what he meant in a lengthy analysis. Perhaps Galileo only knew the passage at second hand; at least, he must not have been familiar with the argument as Aristotle presented it, otherwise such a misunderstanding would have been inconceivable. From another perspective, however, the error is very significant. If Aristotle had indeed meant what Galileo thought he did, then all of natural philosophy in the succeeding two thousand years might have looked considerably different. And if Galileo had embraced, rather than rejected, this

---

cum igitur aer nec gravitatem habeat nec levitatem, a proiciente motus in infinitum movebitur, et semper eadem velocitate; ergo etiam in infinitum portabit proiecta, nec fatigabitur, cum semper eadem vi moveatur. Huius tamen contrarium experientia docet."]

supposed theory, he would have discovered the law of inertia at this early stage of his career.

Galileo came close to making the discovery in another section of the treatise, the chapter entitled "In which the proportions of the motions of the same object on various inclined planes are considered."[21] Here he discusses violent motion that takes place on a hard surface. Assuming that for all practical purposes every source of resistance has been eliminated, that is, that the moving object is a smooth, nondeformable ball and that the surface is hard and polished, then one can say that "any object on a plane level with the horizon will be moved by the least force, and indeed by a force less than any arbitrary force."[22] In this case, only a minimal force would be required to keep the ball in motion. Scholastic thinkers likewise believed that the motive force needed to sustain a violent motion on a horizontal, smooth plane where the resistance of both gravity and friction had been effectively eliminated (and where only the inertial resistance of the ball against the motive force was still operating) is less than in all other situations. But they never concluded that a "force less than any arbitrary force," that is, an infinitely small force, would suffice. Galileo was aware that he was asserting something that his contemporaries would hardly consider credible, for he continues: "And because this seems rather hard to believe, it will be demonstrated with the following argument."[23] But the rather involved proof only shows that such motion can be caused by less force than any motion on an upwardly inclined plane, no matter how small the angle of elevation. Galileo does not say any more on the subject and, in particular, does not address the question of how the motive force continues to operate under the given conditions. It is reasonable to assume, however, that Galileo had in mind here the same general

21. *Opere,* Edizione nazionale 1:296 ff. ["In quo agitur de proportionibus motuum eiusdem mobilis super diversa plana inclinata."]

22. ["Quodcumque mobile super planum horizonti aequidistans a minima vi movebitur, immo et a vi minori quam quaevis alia vis."]

23. ["Et hoc, quia videtur satis creditu difficile, demonstrabitur hac demonstratione."]

principles that he employs in the later chapter on projectile motion. Thus he undoubtedly thought that the impetus would act in exactly the same fashion on a hard surface as it did in the case of projectile motion; that is, it would begin to diminish by itself the moment it came into existence and would decrease continually until it was finally extinguished. This process would take place even though no resistance was present, and the ball would gradually slow down and eventually stop despite the fact that the surface on which it was moving was infinitely large.

*

Galileo returned to the same problem many years later in his *Dialogue on the Two Chief World Systems* [1632] where he considers it in detail. The theoretical approach is, at least in principle, the same as that employed in his youthful treatise. He is still convinced that scholastic impetus theory is correct, and he adopts it unconditionally, without any criticism. At a certain point during the second day's discussion Simplicio reproaches Salviati on this very account: "You have made one assumption throughout this discussion . . . and this is that it is obvious and well known that a projectile separated from the thrower continues to move by means of the force impressed on it by the same thrower."[24] In reality, however, Galileo had already abandoned essential elements of the scholastic theory, even though he obviously had not yet fully realized this.[25]

24. *Opere*, Edizione nazionale 7:175 ["Voi in tutto 'l processo avete fatta una supposizione . . . e questa è il prendere come cosa notoria e manifesta che 'l proietto separato dal proiciente continui il moto per virtù impressagli dall'istesso proiciente."]

25. A letter from Benedetto Castelli to Galileo in 1607 (*Opere*, Edizione nazionale 10:169–71) seems to show that Galileo was already convinced at this time that motion continues by itself. The passage, which has been quoted often, reads: "From your theory, then, that to begin the motion a mover is indeed necessary, but to continue the motion it suffices that there be no opposition. . . ." But the motion in question here and to which Galileo's "theory" applies is celestial motion (understood in the Aristotelian sense). Late scholastic thinkers had already made similar assump-

Earlier in this conversation[26] Salviati uses a sequence of questions to force Simplicio to formulate a law that says that the movement of a ball on a horizontal plane proceeds by itself if all accidental and external sources of resistance have been eliminated. Actually, it is not a horizontal plane that is assumed here, but rather a spherical surface whose center coincides with the earth's center, so that the effect of gravity is completely eliminated.[27] The line of argument is at first identical with that found in the treatise *De motu*. Consider the motion of a ball rolling down a very slightly inclined plane; if left undisturbed, the ball will roll onward with an ever increasing velocity. And if the inclined plane were infinitely large, then the velocity of the ball would become infinitely large. (Note that Galileo has abandoned the idea that the velocity of a falling body at some point reaches a constant value.) And if the ball is moved upward by some impetus violently impressed on it *(qualche impeto violentemente impressale),* then its velocity will immediately begin to decrease and continue to do so until it finally reaches zero. But what will happen if, instead of an inclined plane, there is a horizontal one (or an immense spherical surface) and if some mover imparts to the ball an impetus acting in a particular direction? Will the ball accelerate or decelerate? Simplicio answers that neither will happen, since there is no reason why the velocity should either increase or decrease. To this Salviati replies that if there is no reason why the ball should slow down, then there is even less reason to suppose that it will come to a halt. How long, then, will it continue to move? Simplicio answers, Until it reaches the boundary of the plane. And if the plane were infinitely large, would not the ball's motion likewise be infinite, "without end, that is, perpetual?" Simplicio is compelled to answer, "It seems so to me."

---

tions. Therefore one cannot immediately conclude from Castelli's statement that Galileo intended to advance a corresponding theory for terrestrial motions, especially violent ones.

26. *Opere,* Edizione nazionale 7:171 ff.

27. An impetus can produce both rectilinear and circular motion. This was one of the basic assumptions of the scholastic theory, and Galileo adhered to it throughout his life.

The conversation then turns to other related problems that are of less interest to this discussion. Only one point needs mentioning, and it concerns the relationship between impetus and gravity during the kind of motion just considered, that is, circular motion about a central point *(moto circolare intorno al centro)*. Now, however, the motion is assumed to take place in air rather than on a hard surface. Such conditions arise, for instance, when a stone is allowed to fall from the top of the mast of a moving ship. The stone receives impetus from the ship, and the impetus acts in such a way that the stone follows the ship once it is released. At the same time, however, the stone's gravity impells it toward the center of the earth. Simplicio thinks, in scholastic fashion, that the stone's gravity will offer resistance to the operation of its impetus, but Salviati explains to him that circular motion around a central point and rectlinear motion directed toward the center *(moto retto verso al centro)* do not oppose each other and therefore do not destroy each other. In fact, they can exist simultaneously, since the stone possesses no disinclination *(repugnanza)* toward circular motion; that is, it does not offer any resistance to such motion. Every heavy object has a natural tendency to move toward the earth's center and a natural disinclination toward moving in the opposite direction: "Hence it necessarily follows that in the case of motion which neither approaches nor recedes from the center, the moving object experiences neither repulsion nor attraction; there is, consequently, no reason why the force impressed on it should decrease."[28]

This conclusion differs completely from scholastic impetus theory and from the views of the young Galileo. The impressed force that is imparted to a ball on a horizontal plane or to a stone on the mast of a ship no longer decreases gradually by itself, disappearing altogether after some time. It can, however, be reduced or even destroyed by other forces. But if all external sources of resistance are eliminated, then there is no reason why the impetus should decrease or why the motion it causes should cease. Impetus thus

28. ["Onde necessariamente segue che al moto che non appressa nè discosta dal centro, non ha il mobile nè repugnanza nè propensione nè, in conseguenza, cagione di diminuirsi in lui la facoltà impressagli."]

remains constant if not subjected to external interference and lasts forever, causing uniform motion that likewise lasts forever. Note that here too Galileo's ideas have changed. A moving body unaffected by resistance no longer attains infinite velocity, but rather a motion of infinite duration. In the second passage quoted, the new insight receives further clarification: an object moving horizontally no longer generates an internal resistance against its motion, as scholastic thinkers assumed for every motion. This is so because the material body has no natural tendency to move horizontally as it does to move toward the earth's center, but it also has no natural aversion to horizontal motion and therefore does not seek to avoid it. As a result, the body does not resist the impetus causing it to move horizontally, and this impetus is neither diminished nor destroyed. These theories, however, amount to nothing less than a renunciation of the scholastic concept of inertia, since a material body in a state of uniform motion no longer strives to return to a state of rest. The body now generates no inertial resistance against the impressed force causing its motion, and the impressed force is no longer gradually used up in overcoming this inertial resistance. Under the specified conditions, the impetus and the motion caused by it will actually continue to exist unchanged forever.

In the *Discourses Concerning Two New Sciences* [1638] Galileo continues to advocate the theory of impetus, but he does not develop it in any fundamentally significant way, at least not with regard to the problems considered in this essay.[29] The crucial insights occur in

29. At most it should be mentioned that now instead of circular motion around the center of the earth, Galileo generally considers rectilinear motion occurring on an infinite plane. But this change is not as important as it first appears to be. In the discussions in the *Dialogue on the Two Chief World Systems,* motion on an infinite plane is in no way excluded in principle, but motion on a spherical surface is preferred for the thought experiments because in this case gravity is, for all practical purposes, eliminated, which would only be possible in the abstract for a plane. Moreover, there are also references to motion on a spherical plane in the *Discourses Concerning Two New Sciences.* The circular impetus *(impetus circularis)* of scholasticism has not yet been given up, and the special importance of rectilinear motion has not yet been fully recognized.

the *Dialogue on the Two Chief World Systems,* and I think it not unjustified or exaggerated to view them as the first, implicit discovery of the law of inertia, since they represent an essentially new approach to the inertia of material bodies.

Six:

THE THEORY OF
THE ELEMENTS AND
THE PROBLEM OF THEIR
PARTICIPATION IN COMPOUNDS

In one of her earliest studies, "Die Struktur der materiellen Substanz," first published in An der Grenze von Scholastik und Naturphilosophie *(Essen: Essener Verlagsanstalt, 1943; 2d ed., Rome: Edizioni di Storia e Letteratura, 1952), Anneliese Maier examines in detail the difficulties that arose in the scholastic theory of the structure of material substance and the attempts that were made to resolve them. In the first part of the study she shows that the central problem was how to reconcile the theory of the elements with the metaphysics of form and matter. In the main body of the essay she surveys first the solutions to the problem given by Aristotle and his Islamic commentators, Avicenna and Averroes, and then the explanations offered by thirteenth- and fourteenth-century scholastic thinkers, dividing these latter into two "schools," the Averroistic and the "modern." She concludes the study with the observation that scholastic philosophers did not succeed in reconciling the conflicting theories because the problem, as they formulated it, was fundamentally unsolvable.*

The selection that follows is a translation of only the first part of Maier's study, in which she describes the problem and examines the theoretical background to it. This particular section was chosen both to illustrate Maier's approach and to provide a short but detailed summary of the scholastic theory of the structure of material substance. The text is taken from An der Grenze von Scholastik und Naturwissenschaft, *2d ed., pp. 3–22.*

The structure of material substance has always been one of the most important problems addressed by any natural philosophy or natural science. In every age and for every school of thought the solution to this problem, that is, the theory of the essential nature of material substance, has provided the foundation on which to construct the understanding of inorganic nature and its processes. Indeed, it almost can be said that the answer to this question distinguishes one theory of nature from another. When, at the beginning of the seventeenth century, the decisive change took place in how natural philosophers viewed the world, it was this problem that provided the starting point for modern natural science, as atomism supplanted the medieval doctrine of forms and qualities in attempts to explain the structure of the physical world.

Moreover, the problem is of particular interest for the history of late scholastic natural philosophy and natural science for another reason. Scholastic thinkers were never able to explain how the theory of matter that was axiomatic to their way of conceiving and analyzing nature coincided with their metaphysical assumptions. Their difficulties exemplify in a concrete and clear fashion a process that manifests itself in many forms during the fourteenth century: the gradual weakening and internal breakdown of the medieval world view. The problem itself is of fundamental importance because it concerns the very issue that initiated the momentous transition from the medieval to the modern world picture and because the transition was conditioned to a large extent by the failure of scholasticism to find a solution.

Scholastic philosophy treated material substance in two ways: as a composite *(compositum)* of matter and form and as a compound *(mixtum)* of the four elements—earth, water, air, and fire. The first interpretation derived from scholastic-Aristotelian metaphysics, while the second, the theory of the elements, played a fundamental role in numerous medieval disciplines and was a self-contained, fully developed system. Both theories deal with the question of the structure of physical substance and each offers a solution, but the two answers do not coincide. The metaphysical approach cannot be squared with the viewpoint of natural philosophy. The discrepancy between the two interpretations is revealed in the problem examined in this essay: To what extent is a composite of matter and form at the same time a compound of the four elements?

Scholastic thinkers inherited two possible solutions from Arab philosophy, but both contradicted the basic principles of scholastic-Aristotelian metaphysics. The philosophers of high scholasticism developed a third solution, different from the earlier two, that avoided the difficulties that undermined them, but that did not do justice to the natural philosophical side of the problem. This solution, which saved the metaphysical principles, sufficed at first because problems of natural philosophy and natural science were entirely peripheral to high scholasticism's field of interest. But by the end of the thirteenth century, and especially in the fourteenth century, this attitude changed. Any theory that resolved the conflict between metaphysics and natural philosophy by emphasizing the former and more or less abandoning the latter provoked discussion and attempts to modify it. As a result, the problem became steadily more urgent, while its fundamental insolubility was perceived with increasing clarity. Hardly any other question of natural philosophy attracted so much attention in the fourteenth century. Considerations of natural science had gradually come to play an important role alongside those of pure philosophy, and further progress in many areas depended on the resolution of this problem.

Before the history of the problem itself can be examined, some preliminary observations must be made about the scholastic theory of the elements as such. The discussion that follows is meant to summarize the main points that everyone was familiar with. On the whole, the different schools of thought agreed on this set of general assumptions. Of course, sometimes nuances of interpretation and even differences of opinion arose concerning specific topics, especially when the solution to a particular question had ramifications for some larger issue. But as a rule such disputes did not concern the basic principles considered here.

The theory of the elements was discussed in a variety of contexts. The sources for it can be divided into three classes: philo-sophical, medical, and theological. Foremost among the works on natural philosophy were commentaries on Aristotle's *De genera-tione et corruptione*, which treated the theory in great detail and from every conceivable point of view. Other discussions could be found in the commentaries on *De caelo et mundo* and on the fourth book of the *Meteorologia* and here and there in the commentaries on the *parva naturalia*. Furthermore, pertinent issues were treated in certain chapters of the *Physics* and the *Metaphysics* and some-times in parts of the commentaries on *De animalibus*. In addition, there were numerous independent *quaestiones*, both *quodlibet* ques-tions and ordinary or disputed questions, as well as specialized treatises on the elements and on particular problems concerning the theory itself.

Of the theological sources, special mention must be made of the commentaries on Book II of the *Sentences*, where commentators discussed the Creation and especially the works of the fifth day, when fish and other aquatic animals were brought forth from the waters and birds from the air. This provided theologians with an opportunity to consider in a general fashion the structure of mate-rial substances.[1] Finally, the theory of the elements is found in medical writings on the so-called theory of the humors, particularly in the commentaries on Avicenna and Galen, as well as in the literature concerning the preparation of medicines *(compositio medicinarum)* and in a variety of special treatises. These medical sources, however, are by their very nature oriented toward different kinds of problems. They are less concerned with theoretical expla-nations of inorganic matter than with finding out about the qualities and powers of the elements, their disposition and equilibrium in organic substances, and their effectiveness in inorganic substances. Natural philosophers characteristically inquired into how the ma-terial world is constructed from its ultimate components, but medi-

---

1. As the fourteenth century progresses, however, this source more or less disappears, since in general only the first book of the *Sentences* is still pro-vided with a detailed commentary. But it sometimes happens that the relevant questions are also considered in book 1.

cal writers generally devoted little or no attention to the topic.

The four substances that scholastic-Aristotelian natural philosophers called elements and regarded as the simplest and most basic
forms of matter were earth, water, air, and fire. They were viewed
from two different standpoints: first, as constituent parts of the
universe *(elementa mundi* or *partes mundi)*. This approach, which was
generally developed in the commentaries on *De caelo et mundo,* treats
the elements as independent, concrete physical materials, although
always with the proviso that none of the substances actually ever
exists in a pure, unmixed form. Thus all statements and rules about
them are only valid in the abstractly conceived limiting case of pure
elements.

The most important characteristic of the elements as constituent
parts of the universe is that they are supposed to occupy a spatial
order based on their relative weights. Earth is the heaviest element,
fire the lightest. Between these two extreme elements *(elementa ex-
trema)* are situated the two middle elements *(elementa media),* water
and air (the two "media" of modern physics). Each of the four
elements possesses a natural place corresponding to its position in
this hierarchy. On this point, however, some differences of interpretation existed. One rather widespread notion held that the elements
are arranged in concentric spheres or spherical shells around the
center of the universe, which in scholastic theory coincides with the
center of the earth. Thus the sphere or region of the element earth
forms a ball whose center is the same as the earth's center, and the
region of water forms a spherical shell concentric with the earth and
covering it.[2] Air and fire form further concentric shells, so that the
region of fire is farthest out, lying just beneath the sphere of the
moon.

Pieces of an element that are situated outside their natural place
strive to return there, whence arise the so-called "natural mo-

---

2. But there were also other opinions on this question. In the fourteenth
century the following problem achieved a certain amount of importance:
Does the earth alone form a spherically shaped natural place, or do earth
and water together do this? This idea was, of course, suggested by the actual
conditions found on the Earth's surface.

tions": the downward motion of heavy bodies (that is, free fall) and the upward motion of light bodies (that is, of fire). The attempt to explain such motions in detail raised a number of problems that will be considered later. It should be mentioned here, however, that an element's natural place can also be interpreted in a relative sense. A certain amount of one element is located in its natural place relative to another element when the natural spatial order is adhered to, that is, when the earth is in the lowest position and above it are layers of water, air, and fire. A corresponding interpretation applies to the relative positions of only two or three elements.

The second approach regarded the four elements as the ultimate (so to speak, chemical) components of all physical objects, the basic building blocks from which the material world is constructed. This standpoint was adopted in the commentaries on *De generatione et corruptione*. How, then, was this function interpreted?

Concrete physical substances, the so-called *mixta*, were not thought to consist of certain quantities of the four primary, cosmic materials mixed together. The explanation was sought at a deeper level of material structure. From the perspective of scholastic natural philosophy, the four elements were the ultimate building blocks, but from the perspective of scholastic metaphysics they were not, since the elements themselves are still physical substances and, as such, are composites *(composita)* of form and primary matter like all other material substances. Moreover, all *composita* possess the same universal material substrate:[3] an unformed, purely potential, primary matter.[4] The metaphysical components of any *mixtum* are this primary matter and the form of the compound *(forma mixti)*; in the case of an element the components are

3. Other, divergent opinions postulated internal differentiation of the material, but they were only exceptions to the general view. (Cf. *An der Grenze von Scholastik und Naturphilosophie*, 2d ed. [Rome: Edizioni di Storia e Letteratura, 1952], p. 46 ff., 51 ff., and 58 ff.)

4. The well-known dispute over whether primary matter is purely potential or whether it possesses some minimal activity does not affect this problem.

the same primary matter and the relevant elemental form. Thus the ultimate constituents of the physical world are primary matter and the four elemental forms. The fundamental principle that all higher physical substances must be constructed from the elements means, therefore, that the four elemental forms must be somehow preserved as metaphysical components in the *mixtum*. The explanation of *how* they are preserved was the great problem that scholastic thinkers attempted to solve, first in the thirteenth century and especially in the fourteenth.

The goal of this theory is to construct the world in terms of ultimate, qualitative-formal principles. The notion of ultimate quantitative units is completely lacking.[5] The elemental forms can inform arbitrarily large or small amounts of matter, but the characteristics of the elements remain unchanged. The scholastic-Aristotelian theory of the elements is explicitly opposed to the atomistic point of view.

The detailed description of the four elemental forms is intimately connected with the search for a set of first qualities from which all other qualities derive and that are themselves incapable of further analysis. The reasoning that justifies the existence of such primary, simple first qualities requires that they be tactile qualities, since it is through the sense of touch that the initial physical perception of a body is made. Moreover, they must be active in nature and must, finally, manifest themselves as pairs of opposites.[6] Tactile qualities can be divided into six such pairs of opposites: hot and cold, wet and

5. By this I mean that it was rejected. Scholastic thinkers were completely familiar with atomistic ideas and included detailed discussions of them in their commentaries on *De generatione et corruptione* in connection with Aristotle's rejection of ancient atomism. But it was a rare exception for one of them to adopt such ideas (Nicholas of Autrecourt is the best known example), since the authority both of Aristotle and of the church opposed their reception. The much discussed problem of *minima naturalia*, on the other hand, belongs to an entirely different context. For this topic see *Die Vorläufer Galileis* (Rome: Edizioni di Storia e Letteratura, 1949) p. 179 ff.

6. For this reason light fails to qualify as a first quality, although it is active in nature. Darkness is not the opposite *(contrarium)* of light, but rather its negation.

dry, heavy and light, thick and thin, rough and smooth, and hard and soft.[7] But only those pairs that are active in nature, that is, that are capable of effecting qualitative change, can be regarded as first qualities. The pairs hot and cold and wet and dry satisfy these conditions, and they alone, therefore, constitute the alterative qualities *(qualitates alterativae)*. When a hot object comes into contact with another object it makes it hot, and a wet object makes another object wet. A hard object, on the other hand, cannot make something else hard, nor can a heavy object make something else heavy. The motive qualities, gravity and levity, are therefore excluded from the class of first qualities, although they are undoubtedly active in nature.

These four qualities—hot, cold, wet, and dry—are thus the primary qualities, and as such they must be the qualities of the elements. Four combinations consisting of one quality from each of the two pairs can be formed, and these four combinations suffice for the qualitative description of the four elements. Earth is cold and dry, water is cold and wet, air is hot and wet, and fire is hot and dry. Aristotle and his expositors in antiquity considered this theory to provide a complete ontological definition of the elements. Scholastic thinkers, however, did not agree because the theory only accounts for the accidental forms of the elements, whereas each element has, first and foremost, a substantial form, that is, the form of earth, water, air, or fire. Accidental forms were thought to derive from substantial forms. In other words, the substantial form determines the accidents that belong to it, so that the union of a substantial form with matter necessarily means that the accidental forms are simultaneously introduced. This theory of substantial forms was in a certain sense an elaboration of Aristotelianism developed by the scholastics, since Aristotle did not advocate it, at least not in the distinctive and dominant form it assumed in scholastic metaphysics. The problem of how the elements are preserved in compounds arose primarily from this concept, and it alone explains why a vast

---

7. The seventh pair of opposites listed by Aristotle *(De generatione et corruptione* II, cap. 2), slippery and dry *(lubricum* or *viscosum* and *aridum)*, was usually omitted.

discrepancy existed between the theory of the elements and the general metaphysics of form and matter in scholastic Aristotelianism, when in fact little or no trace of the problem can be found in genuine Aristotelianism.[8]

The substantial form cannot act directly, but only through its accidental forms, insofar as they are active. Here another difficulty arises. Of the four first qualities, Aristotle only considers the pair hot and cold to be active, since cold supposedly has the ability to condense *(congregare)* and heat to separate *(segregare)*. In his view, wetness and dryness only function as passive qualities. Almost all scholastic natural philosophers, on the other hand, agreed that all four first qualities are both active and passive because each one can either act on, or be acted on by, its opposite. Aristotle's position had to be explained somehow, and this was done in a variety of ways, usually be employing the simple distinction that hot and cold are *more strongly* active than wet and dry.

The elements are not permanent, but can be transformed into one another. This notion, which was subjected to particularly heavy criticism by seventeenth-century natural philosophers, is nevertheless a completely logical conclusion based on the principles of the scholastic theory of the elements. It says only that the same lump of primary matter (if I may use such an expression) that is informed by the substantial form of earth at one time can be informed later by the substantial form of water, fire, or air, or by the form of a compound *(forma mixti)*. This assertion is entirely evident in the context of Aristotelian metaphysics. It must, however, be noted that the same lump of primary matter can never be informed by two or more elemental forms *simultaneously*. This conclusion follows from the definition of the elemental form as such and has nothing to do with the controversy that arose con-

8. This also explains why scholastic thinkers always criticized Alexander of Aphrodisias for supposedly identifying the first qualities with the substantial forms of the elements. Of course he did not do this; he simply did not yet have the concept of a separate substantial form. Instead, he (like Aristotle) regarded the totality of the essential accidental forms as the "substance."

cerning the basic acceptance or rejection of multiple substantial forms in the same composite. It is essential to the concept of the substantial forms of the elements that they be capable of being introduced into the same piece of matter successively, although never simultaneously. Everyone, no matter what his school of thought, agreed on this point. The elemental forms are the most basic forms that exist, and they inform primary matter directly. No other preparatory disposition or forming is necessary. It is therefore impossible for a second elemental form to inform a piece of matter that has already received another elemental form. The complete destruction of the previously existing form is a precondition for the introduction of a new elemental form. This remains true whether the previous form was the form of a compound, as in the case of a compound that breaks down into the elements (a process that was always considered to be possible in principle), or if it was an elemental form, as when one element is transformed into another.

Such transformations of one element into another presuppose the existence of certain external conditions. In fact, they are almost exclusively limited to cases in which a large quantity of one element, for instance, water, assimilates a small amount of another, for instance, earth. It was thought possible that a bit of earth immersed in a large amount of water could be transformed into water. The question of how this process of transformation would take place in detail was, however, an issue about which opinions were divided and problems arose; moreover, like other issues of this sort, it was important in other contexts as well. Here the debate centered on the generation of substantial forms, and the main problem was summed up in the question, What causes this generation; in other words, What is the generating agent (*generans*)? In the strict and limited sense of the term, *generatio*, as well as *corruptio*, always referred to the generation or dissolution of substances. Aristotle answered the question unequivocally: the *generans* is simply the assimilating element. Scholastic thinkers, on the other hand, could not accept this solution without modification, since in their view it gave rise to numerous difficulties. It should be clearly understood, however, that the question concerned the transitive cause, that is, the efficient cause that brings about the transformation. What, it was asked, is the effective and productive principle *(principium effectivum et productivum)* of the new substantial form and consequently of the accidental forms or qualities that proceed from it?

First of all, neither the substantial form of the original element nor that of the assimilating element can function as the immediate cause, because a substantial form cannot act by itself, but only through the accidents pertaining to it (insofar as they are active in nature). These qualities, however, only act by virtue of the substantial form with which they are associated. Consequently, the substantial form is only an indirect or remote cause, while the qualities themselves function as direct or proximate causes *(causae immediatae)*. The question immediately arises, Can qualities (that is, accidents) generate a substantial form? Of course, a question such as this was posed not only in relation to the theory of the elements, but also in many other contexts, and it prompted mostly negative answers. Walter Burley was among the minority of thinkers who gave an affirmative response; he believed that accidents could both produce substantial forms and, as a general rule, act on them.[9] But in the great majority of cases such ideas were rejected. At most the possibility remained—and it too was disputed—that the action of the qualities prepares the way for the introduction of the substantial form, that is, that the matter is made ready to accept the new substantial form by the action of the qualities. Thomas Aquinas and some (but not all) Thomists advocated this solution, which became one of the most vigorously disputed points of Thomistic teaching. Generally speaking, the theory asserted that a certain *alteratio* or reciprocal operation of the relevant qualities has to precede the production of the substantial form. The introduction of the substantial form itself, however, does not result from this process and is not caused by terrestrial qualities and forces. At this point a higher

9. Cf. *An der Grenze,* pp. 117–18. Petrus Aureoli (*Sent.* IV, dist. 1. qu. 1, art. 3) also adopted this view, as did the anonymous authors of Vat. lat. 4452 and 2170. (Cf. *An der Grenze* pp. 81–82 and 101 ff.) William of Ockham also accepted it, but with some limitations. (Cf. *An der Grenze,* p. 167.)

power has to intervene, at least according to the most commonly held view, and this power was almost always identified with the celestial forces or the intelligences.[10]

Thus the same intelligences that were supposed to move the heavens were also generally regarded as the generating agents of the elements. Terrestrial substances and forces were excluded from this role. The act of generation in the strict sense, that is, the introduction of the substantial form itself, was thought to take place instantaneously. No motion is involved, as in the preceding preparatory stage *(alteratio)*, because, according to Aristotle, a substance results not from a motion, but from a *mutatio*—a change that occurs in a measureless instant, not during a span of time. This last point also provides an argument for the exclusion of terrestrial forces from a causal role in generation [since no earthly force can produce instantaneous change].

As mentioned, besides the four substantial forms of the elements there are also four accidental forms: the four qualities hot, cold, wet, and dry. All other so-called second qualities derive from these first qualities.[11] There are two classes of secondary qualities: secondary tactile qualities and specific, nontactile sensory qualities.[12] The tactile qualities were listed earlier. They are unusual because they

10. Occasionally, however, one encounters an explicit rejection of this idea. Petrus Aureoli (*Sent.* IV, dist. 1, qu. 1, art. 3) provides a drastic example of this with his candid assertion: "This is the refuge of the wretched in philosophy, just as God is the refuge of the wretched in theology." *(Hoc est refugium miserorum in philosophia, sicut Deus est refugium miserorum in theologia.)* Cf. *Zwei Grundprobleme der scholastischen Naturphilosophie,* 2d ed. (Rome: Edizioni di Storia e Letteratura, 1951), p. 182, footnote 29.

11. One also encounters the designation "secondary qualities" *(qualitates secundariae)* instead of "second qualities" *(qualitates secundae),* for example in the anonymous commentary on *De generatione et corruptione* in Vat. lat. 2185, which is discussed in *An der Grenze,* p. 131. On the other hand, I have never encountered the expression "primary qualities" *(qualitates primariae).*

12. Nicole Oresme refers to these two classes as "second" and "third" qualities in his *Quodlibeta* (qu. 22: *an sint aliquae qualitates secundae et tertiae et quae sint illae;* Florence, Biblioteca Laurentiana, Ashburnh. 210, fol. 54vb–58ra), . . . but this distinction was not usual.

derive directly from the first qualities and are therefore also characteristic of the elements themselves, although since they are not active, they cannot be first qualities. In contrast, the other specific qualities, namely, smell, taste, and color, only result from particular combinations of the first qualities that cannot be produced in the elements themselves, but solely in compounds *(mixta)*. Sound was usually treated as an exception, since it was thought to result solely from local motion, like images. The individual elements have only tactile qualities.

How, in detail, the secondary qualities are generated from the primary ones remained unclear, especially in the case of the specific sensory qualities. Occasionally attempts were made to account for the tactile qualities, for example by deriving hardness from dryness and cold or rarefaction *(raritas)* from heat, but even here much was left unexplained. The derivation of gravity and levity was a particularly difficult topic that, although it was occasionally discussed in detail, was for the most part ignored. In general, no attempt at all was made to account for the specific sensory qualities. Most authors were content to affirm that they arise from mixtures of the first qualities and vary as the component qualities are combined in different proportions. Considered from another perspective, however, the detailed treatment of this question appeared to be superfluous. A compound's secondary qualities were also thought to proceed directly from its substantial form, and therefore no detailed derivation of them based on the mixture of first qualities was necessary. Finally, there was a hybrid solution attributed to Avicenna[13] that postulated that the mixing of the first qualities of the elements in a compound creates a disposition toward the secondary qualities, which nevertheless effectively proceed from the new substantial form.[14]

13. The fourth book of Avicenna's *Naturalia* (Vat. Urb. lat. 186, fol. 133v–150r) deals with qualities. . . . This book had an unmistakable and major influence on the scholastic theory of qualities, not only in this particular matter.

14. In *Die Mechanisierung des Weltbildes im 17. Jahrhundert* (Leipzig: F. Meiner, 1938), p. 4 ff., I indicated that this scholastic theory of first and second qualities can be regarded in a certain sense as a precursor of the

Scholastic thinkers were also acquainted with another way of deriving certain qualities from other ones that played an important role in connection with this problem. It has to do with the relationship between intermediate qualities *(qualitates mediae)* and extreme qualities *(qualitates extremae)*, but it concerns differences in quality rather than intensity. In the case of color, for example, the extremes are black and white and the intermediate colors are red, green, yellow, and so forth.[15] The extremes of taste are sweet and bitter and those of smell are fragrant and offensive *(suave* and *insuave)*; in both instances the gradations between the extremes represent the intermediate sensations. Sounds were either conceived in mechanical terms and therefore not treated in this context or explained with reference to a scale extending from high tones to low.

This notion that intermediate qualities are generated from their extremes found general acceptance. But what does this mean, and how can this idea be reconciled with the theory that the same

---

theory of primary and secondary qualities that seventeenth-century thinkers proposed, albeit on the basis of completely different assumptions, and that Locke in particular popularized. The basic principle is the same in both cases: all other qualities are supposed to derive from a small number of ultimate, primary qualities. But in the seventeenth century the Aristotelian first qualities are replaced by the atomic qualities of figure, size, motion, and number (which coincide with the scholastic-Aristotelian *qualitates communes,* that is, with those qualities that are perceived not only through one sense, but through several). The idea of a subjectivization of the secondary qualities, which in the seventeenth century went hand in hand with the mechanistic outlook, does not appear in scholastic thought, except, perhaps, in the explanation of sounds. The "second qualities" remain completely real, objective factors that are derivative, not primary, only with regard to their origin. At least, this was the dominant interpretation. . . .

15. In the case of color, however, yet another scale of intermediate degrees between the "extremes" of white and black has to be considered: the series of gray tones. In scholastic theory these intermediate gray tones are unusual in that they belong to the same species as the extremes; in other words, this scale is nearly always perceived to be one of intensity rather than quality.

qualities derive from a mixture of the first qualities? The theory does not specify that the extremes of the specific qualities emerge from the first qualities in advance of the intermediate ones in order to generate them.

Scholastic thinkers adopted the theory of the generation of intermediate qualities from their extremes mainly from Aristotle's treatise *De sensu et sensato*. There Aristotle discusses the individual specific qualities one by one and in each case explains how the intermediate quality proceeds from a particular mixture of extremes. Colors, for example, are supposed to derive from mixtures of black and white. But the connection between this theory and the theory that secondary qualities depend on primary qualities is not made completely clear. As frequently happens in Aristotle's works, the reader is presented with two different explanations that do not completely coincide.

Some scholastic writers did more than simply summarize and comment on the relevant passages in Aristotle; they tried to explain away the discrepancy by arguing that the specific qualities, whether extreme or intermediate, are generated from particular combinations of the first qualities.[16] Although in some cases it appears that the intermediate qualities arise from a mixture of the extremes, such as when colors are mixed, these are only mixtures in the accidental sense *(mixtio per accidens)*. The essential process here involves the reciprocal influence and mutual alteration of the first qualities on which the extreme qualities are based, so that the intermediate qualities proceed from the newly created combination of first qualities. Of course, Aristotle's assertion that the intermediate qualities are generated from the extremes and that the extremes persist in the intermediates they generate had to be reinterpreted. This was done by viewing the extreme qualities as parts (so to speak) of the intermediate qualities not in the sense of a causal-genetic compound or a real incorporation, but rather in the sense of a natural affinity between the intermediates and the extremes *(convenientia naturalis*

16. They usually did this in connection with another passage in Aristotle, *Metaphysica* IX, cap. 7 (Bekker 1057 a 18 ff.), where the composition of intermediates from contraries is discussed in a general way.

medii cum extremis). An intermediate quality has a certain similarity to or correspondence with each of the extremes that the extremes themselves do not share. This interpretation does not postulate causal relationships between particular individual qualities, only ontological affinities between species, for within a particular qualitative scale running from one extreme to another, every quality represents a species by itself. The intermediate qualities "contain" the extremes only in this affinitive sense *(secundum convenientiam* or *secundum virtutem).*

Before these introductory remarks are concluded, something must be said about the concept of the *mixtum* as such and its different varieties. A *mixtum* is any physical substance that is not an element. Generally speaking, all material substances or *composita* can be divided into two classes: *elementa* and *mixta.* The latter class, moreover, can be divided into *mixta inanimata* and *mixta animata,* but since they do not differ in material structure, they are considered together in the discussion that follows. *Mixta* are so called because they are mixtures of the four elements. In fact, one of the fundamental principles of this theory requires that every *mixtum* consist of all four elements.[17] The specific characteristics of any particular *mixtum* are determined by the relative proportions of the elements in the compound. This notion reflects the assumption that a *mixtum,* when destroyed, dissolves back into its original, elemental parts.

It is important that the concept of the *mixtio* be correctly understood. Following the lead of Aristotle,[18] scholastic natural philosophers made a general distinction between an apparent compound *(mixtio ad sensum)* and a true compound *(mixtio secundum veritatem).*[19] An apparent compound is made by breaking down the sub-

17. The only exceptions are the so-called *mixta imperfecta,* such as vapors and dry exhalations, that are supposed to consist of water and air in the former case and fire and earth in the latter and that play a role in meteorology in the explanation of precipitation.

18. *De generatione et corruptione* I, cap. 10, 327 a 30 ff.

19. There is also a third case that must be distinguished from the other two, namely, when such a small quantity of one substance is mixed with another substance that it is assimilated. If, for example, a drop of wine is

stances involved into imperceptibly small particles and blending them until the various components can no longer be perceived and thus appear to form a homogeneous whole, although in fact they do not. This kind of mixture was called a *complexio* or a *compositio* to distinguish it from a true *mixtio*, but both labels are misleading, since a *compositium* was something entirely different and the term *complexio* had another, special meaning. A true compound is simply a mixture of the four elements made in such a way that a single, homogeneous substance is created rather than a blend of several substances.[20] This *mixtum* in the strict sense is a composite of primary matter and the *forma mixti*, that is, the substantial form of the compound. Once the compound is created, the same quantity of matter that once consisted of four masses, each informed by one of the elemental forms, is now informed by the form of the compound in such a way that every bit of the new composite is identical in essence *(eiusdem rationis)* with the whole.

How does a true compound come into being? First, there must be a preparatory process similar to the one that produces an apparent compound. The elements to be combined must be brought together and made susceptible to interaction, which can usually be realized only by blending them so that small particles of each component pervade the whole concoction. But these measures only prepare the elements and enable them to interact with each other; they have nothing to do with the actual generation of the *mixtum*. How does this happen; how is the *mixtum* in the strict sense created out of the four elements? This question is related to the problem of how one element is transformed into another and is answered in basically the same way. A preliminary process involving the active qualities of the elements is followed by the introduction of the substantial form

---

mixed with a large quantity of water, then according to Aristotle no compound, not even an apparent one, is produced. Instead, the drop of wine changes itself into water. This process is thus similar to the transformation of one element into another.

20. The *mixtum ad sensum* thus corresponds in principle to the physical "mixture" in the modern sense; the *mixtum secundum veritatem*, to the chemical "compound."

through some higher power. As far as scholastic thinkers were concerned, this account provided a satisfactory solution to the problem of how *mixta* are produced. Of course, a variety of special questions arose that cannot be considered here, but there were no difficulties of a fundamental nature, at least not regarding the creation of the *mixtum*. The really serious problems centered instead on another aspect of the theory: the ontological structure of the *mixtum*.

In the theory of how the elements are transformed into one another, some slight mention was made of the quantities of the elements involved, but the topic was not of central importance. The question of quantity played a greater role, however, in the problem of ontological structure. The diversity of higher substances was supposed to be caused by changes in the proportions with which the elements combined to produce the *mixta*. But how can quantities be involved in what is a purely qualitative synthesis? In raising this question I do not mean to invoke the problem that most authors addressed in this context and that constituted one of the most disputed questions of scholastic natural philosophy: whether matter as such has quantity. On the one hand, it was argued that *quantitas* inheres directly in matter, even though only substantial forms are supposed to inform matter directly, and accidents inhere not in prime matter, but in the *subiectum* (that is, in matter that has already been informed by a substantial form). On the other hand, *quantitas* was regarded as a normal accident that can only belong to a *subiectum*. In any case, all scholastic thinkers, regardless of how they answered this question, agreed that a greater quantity of matter has a correspondingly greater capacity to accept forces and qualities. As unclear as this notion may be, it nevertheless approximates the correct law: that at a fixed level of intensity, a larger mass possesses more force, more capability to act, than a smaller one. In the fourteenth century this idea played a fairly important role in the theory of impetus.[21] Moreover, it even attained exact mathematical formulation in Richard Suisset's concept of the amount of form *(multitudo formae)* or amount of potency *(multitudo potentiae)*, which is clearly distinguished from

21. Cf. *Zwei Grundprobleme*, p. 217 ff.

intensity.[22] Suisset's *multitudo* depends not only on the extension of the subject, that is, on its volume, but also on its material composition, in short, on its mass. This concept of the quantity of force, heat, or other similar attribute, which was at first only latent, found direct expression in the theory of the elements. It was argued, for instance, that three units of earth ought to be capable of exactly three times as much action as one unit because they possess a threefold complement of the active (or first) qualities. Since the activity of these qualities was somehow involved in the generation of compounds, it becomes clear how the quantities of the components could be thought to play a role in what was a purely formal, qualitative process.

But this was not the crucial problem; the essential difficulty lay elsewhere. When one element is transformed into another, the preceding element is completely destroyed, the original substantial form recedes back into the potency of the matter, and the matter is then immediately informed again by another substantial form. This process by itself presents no difficulties. The creation of a *mixtum*, however, is different. Since the *mixtum* is supposed to be formed *from all four elements*, one cannot postulate the destruction of the substances that participate in its creation. The strict interpretation of the theory requires that the elements actually function as the basic building blocks of the physical world. Somehow the elements have to participate in the *mixtum* and retain their formal structure as well. That the matter of the elements becomes the matter of the *mixtum* is obvious and explains nothing. The real question, which sums up the whole problem, is whether the elemental forms are preserved in the *mixtum* and, if so, how. It is thus understandable that this question, posed in the form *utrum substantiales elementorum maneant in mixto,* became one of the most discussed topics of fourteenth-century natural philosophy.

22. Suisset, *Calculationes,* tract. VIII: "De potentia rei" (Venice, 1520).

Seven:

THE ACHIEVEMENTS OF LATE SCHOLASTIC NATURAL PHILOSOPHY

The preceding selections have touched on only two aspects of Anneliese Maier's extensive research: scholastic mechanics and the scholastic theory of matter. Numerous important studies on a variety of other topics were necessarily omitted. Luckily, Maier herself summarized and interpreted the results of her work on scholastic natural philosophy in the essay that follows. In it, she describes the advances that medieval thinkers, especially those of the fourteenth century, made in the study of nature.

The overriding question addressed in the essay concerns the place of scholastic natural philosophy in the history of scientific thought. For Maier, this does not mean merely asking whether any individual modern theories were anticipated in the Middle Ages. Instead, she interprets the question in a much broader sense by asking what changes in attitude and approach contributed to making the fourteenth century an independent but transitional stage between pure Aristotelianism and classical physics. Hence she examines innovations not only in physical theory but also in methodology and world view. The topics she discusses include the scholastic concepts of force and motion; techniques of analysis; the theory of infinity; notions of causality, necessity, and contingency; the inductive method; and the problem of measurement. The medieval theories are, of course, compared to their modern counterparts, but

Maier insists that this step be taken only after the theories have been properly analyzed in the context of late scholastic thought. Only in this way can anachronistic judgments about the modernity of medieval concepts be avoided and the true originality of late scholasticism be appreciated.

This selection is a translation of " 'Ergebnisse' der spätscholastischen Naturphilosophie," which originally appeared in Scholastik 35 (1960): 161–88. *It was reprinted with minor changes in* Ausgehendes Mittelalter, vol. 1 (Rome: Edizioni di Storia e Letteratura, 1964), pp. 425–57; *the translation is based on this text. I have omitted only a section of the introduction in which Maier criticizes theories advanced by E. J. Dijksterhuis and P. Abelé (pp. 427–33). A translation of the original version of this essay appeared in* Philosophy Today 5 (1961):92–107 *under the title "Philosophy of Nature at the End of the Middle Ages," but it contains serious flaws. I have therefore retranslated the essay. Because, however, a section has been omitted, the numbering of the footnotes is new.*

The question of the relationship between late scholastic natural philosophy and the classical physics of the seventeenth century has been discussed for decades and has repeatedly aroused strong feelings. To date no real solution to the problem has been found. The dispute centers on the question of whether and to what extent fourteenth-century thinkers developed theories of inorganic nature and, in particular, explanations of phenomena in the field of mechanics that are "correct" from the perspective of later exact science.

That the natural philosophers of the late Middle Ages went beyond Aristotle in many respects and charted their own course cannot be denied. They transformed and developed some of his teachings, but others they simply rejected and replaced with their own theories. This process began with the reception of Aristotle's writings, that is, with the rediscovery of the works on natural philosophy and the Arab commentaries on them. Robert Grosseteste, Roger Bacon, Albertus Magnus, Thomas Aquinas, and Aegidius Romanus by no means absorbed uncritically the ideas of Aristotle, Avicenna, and Averroes, but at first they limited their criticisms to occasional objections and corrections that usually only concerned matters of pure natural philosophy and physical theory rather than questions of world view.

Not until the fourteenth century did the critique of Aristotle and his commentators really become broader in scope, and as this happened, an independent and original natural philosophy gradually developed. Two centers above all played the leading role in this process: Paris and Oxford. On the Continent were Jean Buridan and his school, in which Nicole Oresme was the most prominent figure, and in England were Thomas Bradwardine and his Mertonians, of whom the most famous were William Heytesbury and Richard Suisset (Swineshead), the "Calculator." Only a short time later a school arose in Bologna around Matthew of Gubbio, and its intellectual and cultural significance resulted in no small degree from its receptiveness to the new theories emanating from Paris and Oxford, which were disseminated throughout Italy from this source at an early date. In the last third of the century two outstanding representatives of the new natural philosophy were active in Germany. Both were products of Buridan's school and had initially taught in Paris: Albert of Saxony, the founder of the University of Vienna, and Marsilius of Inghen, the first rector of the University of Heidelberg.

The cosmology of these "moderns" in fact represents a kind of intellectual revolution that spread rapidly and whose main tenets were almost universally accepted regardless of the conflicts between competing schools of thought. There is no doubt it brought many new ideas into circulation and in many respects directed further development into new channels. But the question that is always asked and that no one can agree on is, Are the insights, postulates, and theories that the fourteenth century adopted in the place of Aristotelianism "correct" in themselves; that is, do they agree with the conclusions arrived at by later research into physics? Moreover, it seems to be widely believed that in answering this question one passes judgment on the value of late scholastic philosophy itself and on the interest that scholars show in it.

This is a peculiar and also completely unhistorical attitude that is almost reminiscent of the Enlightenment. It has its roots in the early research done at the beginning of the twentieth century, which to a certain extent amounted to the discovery of late medieval natural science. Pierre Duhem, who must be credited with having opened up this new field of medieval studies, viewed fourteenth-century "physics" predominantly through the eyes of a natural scientist. He looked for the first glimmerings in the past of later discoveries without paying much attention to the intellectual milieu in which this "physics" belonged and without which it cannot really be understood. Since then much has changed, and scholars have for some time been treating this chapter of intellectual history and the history of science like all others, that is, as the history of ideas or *storia del pensiero,* to use the Italian rather than the German expression. This involves examining the thought of an epoch in its simple historical factuality, without comparing it prematurely to the achievements of later eras or judging what was right or wrong in it. But despite these changes, the old controversy still arises about whether and to what extent the *physici* of the fourteenth century anticipated the theories of later classical mechanics. . . .

In my opinion, the whole question needs to be formulated differently (if it has to be raised at all), so that the achievements and possible historical effects of the new ideas developed in the fourteenth century are not sought solely in their tenuous links to classical physics. Instead, these developments should be examined in a broader context.

The importance of late scholastic natural philosophy, viewed against the general background of the intellectual history of Western Christendom, derives from its new attitude toward nature. It is the first attempt at an independent analysis of nature, one that is initially developed on a purely philosophical level and results, to a certain extent, in a metaphysical and epistemological rediscovery of nature, although not in a mathematical and physical reformulation. This development occurs contemporaneously with the incipient metamorphosis of poetry and visual art that used to be regarded as the first harbinger of the coming Renaissance; it is undoubtedly a component of this process and perhaps a more important one than has been hitherto supposed. From this standpoint, its achievements consist less in transforming the content of the traditional view of nature than in discovering new ways of conceptualizing and comprehending nature. In short, what changes is the method of knowing nature. The attempt is made for the first time to find principles that permit a direct, individual, and empirical perception and understanding of nature, independent of all authority. In doing this, late scholastic thinkers achieved something new and lasting and blazed the trail that succeeding centuries would follow and expand, as scientific research is still doing today.

*

"It is absurd to seek knowledge and the manner of knowing at the same time."[1] The scholastics were fond of citing and commenting on this sentence from the second book of the *Metaphysics,* and it can be applied as a kind of motto to all their original scientific efforts. For although they frequently arrived at astonishing and seemingly modern insights into the "manner of knowing," they did not really exploit the newly discovered methods. Consequently, their positive science remained, with few exceptions, within the general framework of the time. In fact, one gets the impression that they considered it absurd to strive both for knowledge and the manner of knowing and that they therefore consciously limited their efforts to pointing out new directions in the study of nature without intending to pursue them themselves. These new directions, although they belonged to a wide variety of contexts and were discovered in different ways, all have one thing in common: they no longer involve a detour by way of Aristotle's authority. Instead, they lead directly from the experience and reason of the individual to nature and its laws. Reason, many scholastics were convinced, is guided by a "natural inclination toward the truth."

This attitude developed slowly during the thirteenth century as a product of, and hand in hand with, the discussion of Aristotle and his Arab commentators. Aristotelian empiricism, which had almost completely driven out and swept away the Platonism of the twelfth century—at least in the field of cosmology—was gradually trans-

---

1. Aristotle, *Metaphysica* II, cap. 3, in the translation of William of Moerbeke (=I minor, 955 a 13). ["Absurdum est simul quaerere scientiam et modum sciendi."]

formed into an individual empiricism (if I may use such an expression). As it became increasingly apparent that Aristotle was sometimes wrong (and to fourteenth-century thinkers that he was very often wrong), the conviction grew that the same claim to authority asserted on Aristotle's behalf must be granted to other philosophers as well and that the conclusions that other philosophers arrive at by their own methods are just as valid as Aristotle's.

Of course, everything belonging to Aristotelian theory that was not open to criticism and that could be adopted without objection was kept. Unfortunately, this legacy, part of which was received tacitly and part explicitly, included several principles whose acceptance set a priori limits to all the efforts of late scholasticism that no individual was able to surmount. Curiously enough, no one ever attempted a critique of these principles, and the suspicion never arose that they might be incorrect, despite the fact that fourteenth-century thinkers carefully scrutinized the rest of Aristotle's theories before adopting them.

Two of these fundamental assumptions were especially momentous and disastrous. The first is the theory that qualities as such are independent, autonomous factors in natural processes, which, as "intensive magnitudes," figure alongside spatial and temporal magnitudes and, like them, can be regarded as directly measurable and mathematically comprehendible quantities. The whole of scholastic-Aristotelian cosmology derived its character from the role that qualities or, more correctly, intensive magnitudes played in it. Even in the new physics of the fourteenth-century the situation remained essentially unchanged, and all the same disadvantages and difficulties arose, some of which will be mentioned further on.

The second principle is the dictum *omne quod movetur ab aliquo movetur:* every motion requires a particular mover that is connected with it and is its direct cause. Moreover, every normal motion that takes place successively also requires a resistance that opposes the motive force and is overcome by it, since without resistance the result would not be motion but a *mutatio,* that is, an instantaneous change of position. This principle applies to all local motion, even to what is later called inertial motion, and from it derives a whole series of other rules that conflict with classical physics. Some of these rules will be discussed later.

Thus, some of the most important material principles on which fourteenth-century natural philosophy was based were destined from the start to divert the creative energies of scholastic thinkers into the wrong channels, at least as regards *content*. In fact, this burden also becomes noticeable in several places where the *formal* principles of metaphysics and epistemology are considered. On the other hand, scholastic philosophers undoubtedly deserve all the more praise for having nevertheless arrived often enough at correct insights. My objective is to demonstrate in what sense and to what extent this was the case by examining several examples. Of course, it is not within the scope of this essay to investigate everything in detail, so I have selected some of the most important topics that indicate what is new and unusual in the fourteenth century view of nature.

*

I begin with a purely external and formal innovation that was nevertheless of some significance. It is the introduction of a literal calculus (that is, the use of letters in calculations) and its application to problems and proofs that in some way involve quantitative factors that can be used in computations. This new, quasimathematical technique penetrated into every field of knowledge, even the most abstract, and soon became dominant. A whole new discipline came into being, the science of *calculationes*, which inquired into the quantitative or pseudoquantitative aspects of phenomena and processes. A lot of nonsense resulted from this mania for calculation, and it is here in particular that the incorrect assumptions mentioned earlier become noticeable. Scholastic thinkers were convinced that everything in the world that can in some sense be regarded as an "intensive magnitude," whether physical or mental in nature, is just as measurable as spatial magnitudes, and that calculations can be made involving these intensive quantities in exactly the same way as with other quantities. In fact, late scholastic natural philosophy contemplated an extreme and exaggerated quantitative ideal that was not a goal to be attained but a reality already established by a higher intelligence: "You have ordered all things in measure, number, and weight." Scholastic philosophers took this ideal for granted and employed it at will in their speculations.

Despite the overambitious use of this principle, there were two important outcomes. First, it by no means infrequently happened that the *calculationes* were employed in fields that actually were susceptible to mathematical and computational techniques, kinematics being the most important of these. The Oxford school in particular arrived at a number of completely correct solutions to physical problems using calculations. Second, there was the method as such. Fourteenth-century thinkers were, of course, not the first to discover that the quantitative side of physical reality can be considered independently and abstractly. Their innovation consisted in systematically pursuing on a very broad front the elaboration and development of a true methodology, one that survived until the time of Galileo and Descartes.

The same can be said of the method of graphical representation associated with Nicole Oresme, which lived on for centuries in the science of the latitude of forms. This method represented the intensity of qualities and velocities (conceived of as the intensity of motion) as a function of space and time using diagrams with a true coordinate system. (It could be used, for instance, in the case of light intensity that varies in strength from point to point on a surface or that changes over time at one and the same point.) Again, fourteenth-century thinkers were not the first to discover that quantitative proportions of arbitrary variables can be visualized using lines that represent them graphically, but for the first time a true methodology was developed and systematically employed. But just as in the case of the *calculationes,* the new "manner of visualizing" *(modus imaginandi)* was used too ambitiously. All intensive variables (that is, all physical and mental qualities of every kind whatsoever) were of course considered to be directly measurable, and it was assumed that the degree of heat or of whiteness, or even of love or of virtue, could be represented as an exact quantity by a line, just like a distance or a period of time.

Nevertheless, this method, like literal calculus, was also applied to variables that were justifiably regarded as measurable, especially in the field of kinematics. And although it may be true that no new discoveries were made in this way, mainly because the Oxford calculators had already made most of them, the method still provided a clearer means of demonstrating the newly developed theories concerning quantitative relationships. Thus it too survived into the succeeding centuries and was still current at the time of Galileo and Descartes.

These two techniques made fourteenth-century natural philosophy quite different in appearance from that of the thirteenth. The problems considered by high scholasticism and the arguments used to analyze them had been based without exception on Aristotle. The new methods, on the other hand, enabled each individual to ask questions about nature and answer them in his own fashion. The enormous appeal of the *calculationes* in particular (which had a larger field of application than Nicole Oresme's specialized graphical method[2]) can undoubtedly be attributed to the fact that philosophers felt a new freedom from the limitations im-

---

2. This method can perhaps be viewed as foreshadowing other new developments. It is not an anticipation of analytic geometry; despite similarities in the use of graphical representation, Oresme's method is something entirely different. Suppose, for instance, that his *longitudo* represents a spatial extension and that the *latitudines* drawn perpendicular to it represent the intensity of some quality that the object in question exhibits at each point. Oresme does not intend the resulting *curve* to describe the dependence of the intensity on the spatial extension at each point. Instead, he wants the resulting *figure* to portray the physical figure of the quality that, in his view, actually exists (although it is not visible) and to portray it exactly, so that the proportionality is preserved. This is probably the first occurrence of the idea of constructing a true-to-life image of something in nature in a geometrically exact fashion. The same idea underlies the theoretical efforts of fifteenth-century thinkers to develop a "scientific" artificial perspective. Whether there might be an actual connection between the two is a question I will leave to art historians, although it is certain that Oresme's method was widespread and well known at the time of Leon Battista Alberti and Piero della Francesca. It is not possible to discuss here once again the extent to which Oresme's statements in the last chapter of his treatise may be viewed as a discovery of graphical integration. For this see *An der Grenze von Scholastik und Naturwissenschaft*, 2d ed. (Rome: Edizioni di Storia e Letteratura, 1952), p. 338 ff., and *Zwischen Philosophie und Mechanik* (Rome: Edizioni di Storia e Letteratura, 1958), p. 373 ff.

posed by the standard Aristotelian questions and modes of demonstration, so that they enjoyed, as it were, a new independence.

But in reality the increasingly abundant literature of the later fourteenth, fifteenth, and even sixteenth centuries, although it is full of *calculationes* of every kind and diagrams like Oresme's wherever appropriate, did not make any substantial improvement over the discoveries made by Heytesbury and Suisset in the 1330s. The later writers were clearly not at all intent on extending their knowledge into other, more general fields by means of calculations. In fact, just the opposite was true: they were only interested in posing the most complicated, specialized problems possible so that they could work them out using all the refinements of the technique. The great achievement and, as it were, the victory over Aristotle consists in the method itself. The interesting thing is not the knowledge *(scientia)*, but rather the manner of knowing *(modus sciendi)*.

*

The problem of infinity is another topic that underwent a basic change in approach during the fourteenth century. In the field that later came to be called infinitesimal calculus, scholastic philosophy made several discoveries of fundamental importance. Here too a new "manner of knowing" nature was involved: infinity and the infinitesimal were brought into the realm of the comprehensible. A less important, but still interesting and fruitful aspect of this development was the debate over the possibility of an existing infinity, for instance, an eternity of past time *(aeternitas ab ante)*. The discussion of such metaphysical questions may have prepared the way for certain kinds of philosophical speculation that appeared later,[3] but it was not crucial for the understanding of nature. Two other factors were much more significant: the inclusion of infinite and infinitesimal magnitudes in the natural world itself and the growing conviction that they could be employed in calculations like normal finite magnitudes.

3. Once the existence of a spatial infinity or an infinite past or future is accepted as a *possibility*, then only one more step is needed to postulate its reality.

One important step in the first direction, for example, was the replacement of the *instans* (that is, the measureless moment in time) by a differential with respect to time. As a result, motion taking place without resistance was no longer considered to happen instantaneously *(in instanti)*, as both Aristotle and the thirteenth-century scholastics had supposed, but rather in an infinitely small span of time or, in other words, with infinite velocity. Likewise, the dimensionless point was replaced by an infinitely small spatial magnitude in numerous problems in which difficulties had arisen because, as the scholastics correctly understood, even an infinite number of points cannot make the smallest finite magnitude. In the second area, the very popular fourteenth-century discussions about the possibility of a creation from eternity *(creatio ab aeterno)* and about the structure of the continuum convinced at least several philosophers that one infinity can be larger than another. For instance, given that the world has existed eternally in the past, it follows that more months have gone by than years although the number of both is infinite. Conversely, these philosophers concluded that one *indivisibile* (that is, one differential) can be smaller than another. In short, they recognized that infinitely large and infinitely small quantities are subject to the rules of arithmetic just like finite quantities.[4]

This is, of course, a considerable improvement on Aristotelian philosophy, which only allowed a potential infinity *(infinitum in fieri)* and assumed that all infinities are alike. Yet once again, scholastic thinkers stopped short with the discovery of the new "manner of knowing" and did not use it to gain new insights. In other words, they did not discover differential and integral calculus. Although here and there in a particular problem some thinker realized that the quotient of two infinite magnitudes can be finite or that the product of an infinitely large and an infinitely small magnitude can

4. What they did not grasp, however, although the insight was sometimes close at hand, was the distinction between infinite sets that is later called their cardinality. Scholastic thinkers were convinced that the series of whole numbers tends toward the same infinity as the multitude of points in the continuum or, in modern terms, that continua are countable sets.

also be finite, no general rules were formulated and no calculations were made.[5] What the philosophers did accomplish, however, was to incorporate infinity and infinitesimals into the realm of the mathmatically conceivable, and this was certainly one of the seeds of later developments.

*

Without a doubt it was Thomas Bradwardine who, in his *Tractatus proportionum*, published in 1328, anticipated to the greatest extent the methodology of the natural science of the future.[6] His discovery of the mathematical function as a tool for describing with exactitude relationships of physical dependence was universally recognized and accepted with incredible speed. The actual formula that Bradwardine developed and that embodies the principle of his discovery is, however, completely incorrect in content. But this does not reduce the value of the discovery itself one bit. Bradwardine's only concern was to express the fundamental laws of Aristotelian dynamics in the form of a universally applicable rule, not to discuss the substantial validity of these principles. His result is therefore in many respects necessarily false, but in its formal aspect it is entirely correct. Like all his contemporaries, Bradwardine stopped short of criticizing Aristotle's dictum *omne quod movetur ab aliquo movetur* and the consequences that derive from it. Every motion arises from the action of a motive force against a resistance; if they are equal (or if the resistance is greater), no motion occurs. Only if the force is able to overcome the resistance does the body move, and its velocity depends on the degree to which the motive force exceeds the resistance. None of these assumptions was questioned. The only matter

---

5. On the other hand, already in the fourteenth century a number of important discoveries were made in what is later called set theory. We need only mention the equivalency principle, which Albert of Saxony, for example, stated quite clearly, or the principle that is later formulated as the so-called Dedekind Cut. Cf. *Die Vorläufer Galileis* (Rome: Edizioni di Storia e Letteratura, 1949), chap. 7.

6. For the details see *Die Vorläufer Galileis*, chap. 4 [translated in part in chap. 3 above] and *Metaphysische Hintergründe der spätscholastischen Naturphilosophie* (Rome: Edizioni di Storia e Letteratura, 1955), p. 373 ff.

of opinion was the mathematical relationship used to describe them.

The excess of force over resistance can be conceived either geometrically or arithmetically; that is, it can be expressed either as a quotient *(proportio)* or as a difference. Furthermore, the velocity's dependence on this quotient or difference can take on various forms. Aristotle and Averroes thought of the excess of motive force over resistance as a quotient and defined velocity as a magnitude proportional to this quotient, provided that the force is greater than the resistance.[7] In the case of equilibrium, when $p = r$ (where p is the *potentia activa* or motive force and r the resistance), the velocity *(v)* is zero. This was also the dominant approach in high scholasticism, although other possibilities were sometimes taken into consideration. But the theory advanced by Aristotle and Averroes suffers from one difficulty: if the velocity is made proportional to the quotient of force and resistance $(v = p/r)$,[8] then the rule says that $v = 1$ in the case of equilibrium, when $p = r$. But the physical assumptions require that $v = 0$, and this, of course, also squares with experience. Up until the 1420s no one was bothered by this discrepancy. The proportionality proposed by Aristotle and Averroes was accepted without question, and no one took issue with the fact that in this analysis the transition from rest to motion must occur with quite a jump, since as soon as the force exceeds the resistance, even by an imperceptible amount, the velocity must immediately take on a value greater than 1. On the other hand, one of the basic principles of scholastic cosmology said that nature does not make jumps and that every change happens continuously and, in modern terms, with continuity, so that every intermediate stage is passed through. High scholasticism tacitly accepted this absurdity that resulted from its fundamental laws of mechanics. Its philosophers apparently viewed the state of rest that occurs when $p = r$ and the process of motion $(p > r)$ as two independent phenomena that could be considered separately.

7. Aristotle still considered each case individually and did not employ the concept of velocity in this context. (He speaks of the distance that an object traverses in a certain time.) Averroes was the first one to formulate the rule in the way that becomes traditional in high scholasticism.

8. For the sake of simplicity, the proportionality constant is set to 1.

At this point Bradwardine enters the picture and postulates that the relationship between velocity and the quotient of force and resistance must be the same for all values of the quotient, that is, for all values taken on by the independent variables. The Aristotelian theory that the relationship is one of simple proportionality must therefore be false and must be replaced. Thus, Bradwardine became the first person in the history of physics to demand that natural processes that exhibit continuity be described by a corresponding mathematical function.[9] The actual rule that Bradwardine then developed is highly complicated. When expressed as a modern equation it reads $n \cdot v = (p/r)^n$, where n is an arbitrary parameter. In explicit form it becomes $v = c \cdot \log (p/r)$.[10] What he discovered is a formula that in fact satisfies the given requirements: the velocity changes continuously as the quotient p/r varies, the value of v stays positive as long as the force is greater than the resistance, and (what

9. Werner Heisenberg ("Die Plancksche Entdeckung und die philosophischen Grundfragen der Atomlehre" in *Jahrbuch der Max-Planck-Gesellschaft*, 1958, p. 26) saw the true essence of Newtonian mechanics, the source of the extraordinary influence of his *Principia* on the thought of succeeding centuries, in the fact that "for the first time natural phenomena could be described mathematically as temporal processes." But this statement can be applied almost verbatim to Bradwardine's discovery.

10. c is an arbitrary constant. [Maier's first equation, $n \cdot v = (p/r)^n$, is meant to express the essential insight of Bradwardine's rule, but it is not, in fact, a mathematical formulation of that rule. For instance, when $p = r$ and $n = 1$, it gives $v = 1$, not $v = 0$. The equation is probably intended to be a shorthand version of this statement: Bradwardine discovered that if the quotient p/r is greater than zero and produces a velocity v, then the velocity $n \cdot v$ (for $n > 0$) will result from a quotient of force and resistance equal to $(p/r)^n$. Cf. Maier's discussion in *Metaphysische Hintergründe*, p. 374. What Bradwardine was looking for was a function $v = f(p/r)$ that satisfies the condition that $n \cdot v = f[(p/r)^n]$ is > 0 when $p/r > 1$. Expressed in this notation, Bradwardine's rule becomes $n \cdot v = n \cdot f(p/r) = f[(p/r)^n]$. Maier recognized that the logarithmic function can be substituted for the unknown function f, since $n \cdot v = n \cdot \log(p/r) = \log[(p/r)^n]$. Consequently, in explicit form Bradwardine's equation becomes $v = \log(p/r)$ or, as Maier puts it, $v = c \cdot \log(p/r)$.]

is most important) when $p = r$, the formula gives $v = o$ and not $v = 1$. The dependence of velocity on force and resistance is thus expressed by a function that is, in fact, valid for all values of the variables without exception.

In content, as a law of nature, Bradwardine's formula is just as false as the physical assumptions on which it is based. But in its formal aspect it represents a great and revolutionary achievement. Bradwardine was fully conscious of this: "Now that the clouds of ignorance have been driven away by the winds of demonstration, it only remains for truth to shine forth with the light of knowledge." With these words he announces, after having rejected several other solutions, his new discovery. And it is no exaggeration to say that he discovered the same methodological principle that would later become the most important and universal tool of modern physics.

The importance of the discovery was reflected in its effect: it was quickly disseminated far and wide and won general acceptance. It obviously solved a problem that others had addressed, and it filled a gap that had been generally perceived to exist. Soon after the publication of the *Tractatus,* Bradwardine's formula was employed in every possible way and in every field of knowledge, especially in the *calculationes* literature, which modeled a large part of its problems directly on this new discovery. But even in philosophy and theology, particularly in commentaries on Aristotle and the *Sentences,* one comes across Bradwardine's function again and again in the most diverse contexts well into the sixteenth century. It gradually became the standard method of describing relationships in which somehow (and the possibilities are numerous) one magnitude depends on the *proportio* or quotient of two others, even when there was hardly any similarity to the original problem that first prompted Bradwardine's discovery. Again, it was the method itself that made the principal impact and took on a life of its own.

*

Bradwardine's reform of dynamics was not the only effort whose content was adversely affected by the adherence to Aristotle's principle "everything that is moved is moved by something." This axiom also paralyzed a new concept of motion that contained an important new perspective and might have made possible the discovery of the law of inertia if the Aristotelian impediment had not been in the way. More precisely, the law of inertia would have followed as a logical consequence from this new idea of motion if the conclusions derived from it had not been twisted to conform to the Aristotelian rule. The new explanation of local motion came from Buridan, and for the first time local motion was divorced in principle from those other "motions" of Aristotelian philosophy, quantitative and qualitative change. Buridan rejected both the traditional concept and Ockham's interpretation and regarded local motion as an independent flowing (*fluxus*) that inheres in the moving object like a kind of qualitative accident.[11] On closer analysis, it appears to be somewhat analogous to a state (*status*), which is how classical physics views motion. But Buridan did not dare to draw the obvious conclusion from his definition of local motion. If motion is an independent and "absolute" accident of the moving body that (1) is to be conceived of as something analogous to a quality, (2) like a quality has an intensity (the velocity), (3) can undergo inten-

11. Ockham adhered to the traditional point of view that identified motion with the *forma fluens*, that is, with the *termini motus* (so that local motion, for instance, was identified with "flowing place"). He only took this approach to its ultimate conclusion. But it was impossible for Buridan and his successors to build the kind of philosophical system they had in mind using a concept of motion in which the basic element of flowing (*fluere*) was suppressed and which saw in local motion only the object, the *termini motus*, and the fact that the object does not occupy two *termini* at any one time. The Oxford philosophers, whose interests lay more in calculations and the mathematical aspect of the problem, were satisfied with this concept of motion and adhered to it. The Parisian school, however, completely rejected it. In and of itself the idea of local motion that Buridan proposed as a substitute for Ockham's was nothing new. It had already been described in detail by Avicenna, but had nearly always been rejected as a philosophical theory. On the other hand, it corresponded to the "opinion common to all" (*opinio communis omnibus*). Ockham mentioned it in this regard, that is, as the view of the *vulgus*, the man in the street. Buridan was the first one to make it into a scientific concept (or, more correctly, to make it into one again), and it became one of the cornerstones of his new physics.

sion and remission (acceleration and deceleration), and (4) could even exist, just like sense qualities, without a *subiectum,* that is, without an object, through God's omnipotence (Buridan assumes all this), then it would have been logically consistent for him to draw the same conclusions for local motion as apply to qualities, namely, that once created it is independent from its cause and exists until destroyed by external forces. This would have constituted the discovery of the law of inertia. Another philosopher, Blasius of Parma,[12] who lived somewhat later in the fourteenth century and in other ways disregarded many of the traditional obstacles, actually took this last step, although he did not pursue its implications. Nevertheless, he stated the conclusion clearly and unmistakably and can therefore definitely be regarded as the first discoverer of the law of inertia.[13]

In Buridan's case, however, Aristotle's principle "everything that is moved is moved by something" interposed itself between him and this conclusion. He could not free himself from this assumption, and it not only blocked the route to a new discovery but also created an additional problem. Buridan defined motion as an absolute accident, but how was this definition to be related to a mover so that each momentary state of the motion depends exclusively on the motive force causing it and not at all on the immediately preceding state? This is an idea whose approximate analogue in modern physics is found in the explanation of electricity, for instance, in the operation of an electric light. At every instant the brightness depends directly on the electric current flowing through it; that is, the intensity of the light varies with the intensity of the "force" producing it, and the illumination disappears immediately when the force ceases to operate (in other words,

---

12. Cf. *Die Vorläufer Galileis,* p. 19 ff., and *Zwischen Philosophie und Mechanik,* p. 140 ff.

13. That is, unless one wants to regard Peter John Olivi as the absolutely first discoverer, since he arrived at a basically similar solution using a completely different line of argument. For more on this see *Ausgehendes Mittelalter,* vol. 1 (Rome: Edizioni di Storia e Letteratura, 1964), p. 359 ff., *Metaphysische Hintergründe,* p. 355 ff., and *Zwischen Philosophie und Mechanik,* chap. 6. [The first reference is translated in chap. 4 above.]

when the current is turned off). Once produced, the illumination does not maintain itself until destroyed by external factors, but only exists as long as its cause exists.

Buridan conceived of motion in just this fashion, as he himself clearly reveals in his discussion of how to explain the intension and remission of local motion, that is, acceleration and deceleration. Scholastic philosophers had proposed numerous theories to provide an ontological account of the changes in intensity shown by qualities; the two most important were the addition theory and the succession theory. The former argued that an increase in intensity results from the addition of new degrees of intensity to those already present, while the latter maintained that the intensities succeed one another, that is, that at one moment the current intensity is destroyed and in the next moment a completely new, stronger intensity is generated in its place. Remission was explained in a corresponding fashion, with degrees being subtracted or a weaker intensity being generated. The succession of forms in the latter theory was thought to happen in such a way that each momentary state does not proceed from the previous one but only follows and displaces it. Now, Buridan's interpretation is very revealing. In the case of permanent qualities he advocated the addition theory: when, for instance, heat undergoes intension, the degree of warmth present at a given moment is maintained into the next one, and new degrees of warmth are added to it and fuse with it. But in the case of local motion he favored the succession theory: the individual momentary velocities succeed one another but do not proceed from one another. There is no direct continuity between the different momentary states of a local motion; each one depends only on the cause at that moment, that is, on the motive force. The continuity of the whole process is based simply on the continuous existence of this force, which is, of course, itself a permanent quality. In this way the idea of motion as an independent accident was made to conform to the dictum "everything that is moved is moved by something," but at the same time a new, forward-looking concept was deflected back into the traditional channels.[14]

14. For the details see *Zwischen Philosophie und Mechanik*, chap. 3.

In itself, the principle that every motion presupposes a motive force presented no obstacle to the rise of classical physics or to the discovery of the law of inertia. Many seventeenth-century philosophers and physicists—all, probably, who were not Cartesians—conceived of motion in principle as the result and not the cause of forces and traced all movement in the last analysis back to innate forces *(vires insitae)* or *impetus* that had been imparted to the ultimate particles at the creation of the world. These forces were the source first of the movement of the atoms and then, more generally, of every other local motion. But anyone who therefore concludes that Buridan's impetus theory must somehow have contained the first glimmerings of the law of inertia has overlooked the essential point that makes all the difference.[15] It can be formulated in scholastic terminology as follows: the seventeenth century attributed detached motions *(motus separati)* ultimately to *vires infatigabiles,* that is, to universal, indestructable, inexhaustible, and unchangeable forces, while Buridan postulated for every motion of this kind a finite, limited, temporary impetus that functions as a particular and ad hoc cause of motion and, most important, is a *vis fatigabilis* used up in moving the object. Buridan could have deduced from his new concept of motion a version of the law of conservation that would have been similar to Descartes' formulation, if he had been consistent and had regarded local motion as a state that maintains itself like a permanent quality. But he could not and did not take this step because of his assumptions.

Likewise, in principle Buridan could have proceeded from his theory of impetus to the discovery of a law of inertia that would have approximated the formulations of Galileo, Leibniz, and Newton, if only he had conceived of the impetus imparted to the projectile by the hand as an inexhaustible force *(vis infatigabilis),* just like the impetus that he had suggested God imparted to the celestial bodies at the creation of the world. In this case the conclusion would not have been that motion as such can maintain itself in the same state unless disturbed by an external force, but

15. J. Abelé [advocates this view] in a review of P. Duhem, *Le Système du Monde,* vol. 8, which appeared in the *Archives de philosophie* 21 (1958): 603 ff.

rather that an imperishable and indestructible impetus can produce uniform motion of infinite duration. But Buridan did not
and could not take this step either. His theory of impetus did postulate an analogue to the law of inertia of classical physics, but it
applied only to celestial motions, not terrestrial ones.[16] He theorized that the impetuses that move the heavens act as the organs
and instruments of the first mover and are therefore *vires infatigabiles;* that is, they draw on an unlimited source of energy and
transform it into motions of infinite duration. Terrestrial impetus,
on the other hand, always represents a finite source of energy and
only acts until this energy is used up. This difference between
exhaustible and inexhaustible forces separates Buridan's terrestrial
impetus from the innate forces that the seventeenth century used
to explain the motion of the ultimate particles.

Little attention had been paid to the theory of the inexhaustibility
of forces, even though it played a considerable role in scholastic
mechanics and contains an important and fundamental discovery.[17]
The concept of motive force *(vis motrix)* was one of the most obscure
in scholastic philosophy, and, in fact, it was never really given a
systematic explanation. Motive force was a special kind of active
quality whose function was not, like other forces, to assimilate its
object, but rather to move it. The "something" in the Aristotelian
dictum "everything that is moved is moved by something" was first
and foremost simply an animate force, and thus it included a variety
of elements not susceptible to mathematical formulation. Basically
this was still true in the new physics of the fourteenth century.
Socrates can use his motive force either directly, by moving an
object that is in contact with him, or indirectly, by imparting an
impetus, that is, an offshoot of his own motive force, to an object
he throws. Let us disregard the second alternative for a moment.

In the normal case of motion resulting from continuous contact
(motus coniunctus), Socrates uses up his force, which "is fatigued"

16. Cf. *Ausgehendes Mittelalter* 1:364 ff. [translated in chap. 4 above], and
Zwischen Philosophie und Mechanik, p. 370 ff.

17. For the details see *Metaphysische Hintergründe*, chap. 4.; cf. also *Zwischen
Philosophie und Mechanik*, chap. 4.

(fatigatur) and after a while dies out. It is regenerated, however, after Socrates takes a rest. The phenomenon of fatigue *(fatigatio)* led fourteenth-century thinkers to distinguish two components in motive forces, and although at first this distinction was still somewhat unclear and sometimes even entangled in contradictions, it shows that their insight was both important and correct. To put it briefly, they discovered the difference between energy and force; that is, they saw that in the process of motion something in the mover is consumed materially, so to speak, while another, more formal component causes and regulates this consumption or transformation of energy into motion. This discovery then led to the distinction between exhaustible and inexhaustible forces *(vires fatigabiles* and *infatigabiles)*, between motive forces that—if I may put it this way— have at their disposal a finite or infinite amount of energy and can correspondingly cause motion of finite or infinite duration. All animate motive forces and the impetus deriving from them belong to the first group, while the second group comprises all celestial movers and forms of impetus deriving from them, namely, gravity and levity. But their explanation goes beyond the scope of this essay.

The distinction of energy and force components in the traditional concept of motive power represents a completely new idea not found in Aristotelianism. If it had been developed in greater detail, it might have produced new insights. But once again, fourteenth-century thinkers did not pursue these possibilities, and here, as in their theory of impetus, they only pointed out the way to a new science without traveling it very far themselves, much less following it to the end.

*

In the areas from which the examples were drawn so far—the mathematical description of natural processes and the foundations of mechanics—all the "results" fourteenth-century philosophers achieved have had a somewhat relative character, since the new initiatives were repeatedly brought to a halt by the traditional beliefs that late scholasticism was not yet able to overcome. There are, however, other types of problems in which these obstacles were not involved, and here one can actually discover a number of "correct" results. The particular areas of philosophical innovation include causality and the causal principle, necessity and contingency, and finality and the laws of nature. Here late scholastic thinkers arrived at some surprisingly modern insights.

The principle that every cause in sufficient contact with a suitable object acts with necessity, and, conversely, that every effect of a transitive cause[18] is likewise produced necessarily, was a well-established axiom that was generally cited in the especially precise formulation given it by Avicenna. But another notion of *necessitas* had pushed in alongside and in front of the established one during the period of high scholasticism, causing considerable confusion about the concept, and it was not until the fourteenth century that philosophers found a solution to the problem. The confusion resulted from the Aristotelian concept of necessity *(ut semper)* and the related notions of contingency *(ut frequenter)* and chance *(ut raro)*. A cause acts with *this* kind of necessity if and only if the effect always occurs; an example of this is the daily rising of the sun. If, on the other hand, a cause only produces an effect in most cases, but not always, then it acts contingently. Finally, if the effect is only observed in a minority of cases, then it is a matter of chance. A favorite example of *ut frequenter* is the person born with five fingers, while someone with six fingers represents a case of *ut raro*. Having five fingers is not an effect that occurs *ut semper*, that is, with real, absolute necessity, although, on the other hand, it was taken for granted that the five fingers are produced by their cause with the natural necessity of Avicenna's principle.

The modern reader of the pertinent texts has no trouble characterizing and classifying ontologically these concepts of necessity and contingency. What is obviously involved here is not the necessity or contingency with which the efficient cause as such acts, but rather the probability with which the expected effect occurs. *Ut semper* corresponds to a probability of 100 percent, *ut frequenter* to more than 50 percent, and *ut raro* to less than 50 percent. In modern

18. The transitive cause does not necessarily have to be the immediate cause, since in certain circumstances it can be at the head of a long causal chain, but it must always exist.

terms, this necessity is simply a statistical necessity, while the other kind, which the Avicennan principle of causality attributes to the operation of the cause itself, is a dynamic necessity. The situation became complicated because statistical necessity was referred back to the causes, and, as a result, people began to inquire into the characteristics of efficient causes that act with this kind of necessity as opposed to others that act contingently. Now, since there are also "contingent" causes in another, metaphysical sense, namely, decisions based on free will, whose contingency has nothing to do with the notion of *ut frequenter*, a considerable muddle ensued, and the fact that fourteenth-century thinkers restored clarity here is an accomplishment that should not be underrated.

The details of the solution cannot be given here,[19] but the upshot was that the principle of causality was declared to be universally and unconditionally valid: every cause acts with absolute necessity, and, conversely, this necessity is the only one that should be labeled as such. Even processes that only occur *ut frequenter* result from their causes with this absolute necessity, since—and this is the fundamentally important insight—when an agent is partly obstructed or when other agents negate its effects, the totality of positive and negative causes, taken together, can be regarded as the efficient cause of the effect produced, which of course follows from the cause so defined with absolute necessity. Fourteenth-century natural philosophers recognized that it makes no sense to talk about "obstructive causes" *(causae impedibiles)* and to attribute to them only a contingent effect, as thirteenth-century thinkers had done, because the obstructions are partial causes just as much as the partially obstructed principle cause. Basically this is all clarification of terminology rather than metaphysical revaluation of the concepts of necessity and contingency. But this clarification also represents the introduction of a methodological guiding principle that characterizes the cosmology of Buridan, his immediate students, and those more remote from him.

At about the same time that this examination of necessity and contingency was being made, but independently and in the context

19. See *Die Vorläufer Galileis,* chap. 8.

of other problems, the same thinkers began to insist on another methodological abstraction that points in the same direction: the exclusion of final causes from the description of the physical world. This is not to say that Buridan and his successors intended to deny the operation of final causes in natural processes. Such an idea would never have occurred to them. But they arrived at the insight that—to phrase it in modern terminology—physics can be abstracted from final causes and that it is advantageous to do so for methodological reasons. It was a fundamental law, originally stated by Aristotle and repeatedly reaffirmed by thirteenth-century thinkers, that every final cause requires or assumes a corresponding efficient cause. A final cause never acts directly or "head on," but always in an indirect fashion or "from behind" by means of an efficient cause. In this regard, fourteenth-century thinkers did not discover anything new or throw any traditional ideas overboard. But once again, they clarified some rather confused concepts and thereby contributed significantly to a broader understanding of nature.

It appears that Buridan was the one who took the crucial step by recognizing that the principle of causation suffices for the explanation of natural processes and that the final causes to which the efficient causes correspond can be ignored. The key idea here is that particular causes always operate in the same fashion under the same conditions, and their modes of operation conform to certain fixed rules. From this insight it immediately follows that every causal relation that occurs in nature proceeds unambiguously and determinately from its starting point and that any reference to an end or any explanation based on a purpose or goal is superfluous. In other words, Buridan replaced final causes as the explanatory principles of physics with laws of nature.[20]

This insight was linked to another that was equally important, namely, the recognition of induction as a fundamental element of scientific methodology. Here too, a significant advance over high scholasticism was made. Of course, it was known as early as Albertus Magnus and Roger Bacon that in the last analysis Aristotle had arrived at certain principles of his cosmological system by induction

20. For this development see *Metaphysische Hintergründe*, chap. 5.

alone. But not until the fourteenth century was an original and independent theory of induction developed in addition to, and sometimes in place of, Aristotelian induction. Its advocates claimed for it, and by implication for the inductive method as such, the same validity granted to the Aristotelian approach.

The situation was brought to a head by Nicholas Autrecourt,[21] who maintained that only those things ensured by the principle of contradiction are knowable. In other words, only that which is absolutely evident in the sense that its converse entails a contradiction is knowable. This meant in particular that all statements about substances and about causal relationships were deprived of cognitive value. It is hard to say whether Autrecourt really intended to advocate, in the manner of Hume, a positivism of pure experience that follows from such an approach ("I am clearly certain of the objects of the five senses and of my actions"); or whether here, as in other instances, he merely wanted to polemicize against everybody and everything. In any case, it is certain that Buridan took this attitude as an attack on the method that he himself proposed to use, at least in principle, to construct a philosophy of nature, and he reacted accordingly. In his debate with Autrecourt, Buridan did not attempt to refute his opponent by proving that substances and causal relationships can be known with complete certainty; he undoubtedly would have conceded this point to him. Instead, he directed his attack against Autrecourt's methodological axiom that the principle of contradiction is the sole criterion of certainty and against his assertion "that there are no degrees of certainty about whether something is correct." Buridan undoubtedly recognized various levels of scientific certitude[22] and would have considered it

21. For Buridan's concept of induction and his polemic against Autrecourt, see *Metaphysische Hintergründe*, p. 384 ff.

22. This conviction also explains, in another context, the attitude of Buridan and his students toward the problem of double truth. Counterposed to the highest and irrefutable evidence, which is guaranteed by divine revelation, there is another kind of certainty found in "philosophical truth." In the last analysis it is acquired through induction and is therefore always only a relative certainty, having more the character of probability than of truth. (Cf. *Metaphysische Hintergründe*, chap. 1.)

useless to demand mathematical exactitude in fields such as the natural and moral sciences. Here it suffices to have adequately confirmed experience, which is to say that it suffices to use the inductive method, the "drawing together *(inductio)* of many particulars, through which the intellect, although it does not see what is immediate or the rationale for what is immediate, is driven by its natural inclination toward the truth to admit *(concedere)* a universal proposition."[23]

Moreover, Buridan explicitly emphasizes that it is experimental induction *(inductio experimentalis)* that he has in mind, by which he means induction that proceeds not only from the observation of daily life, but also from the results of planned experiments. The examples he introduces to illustrate this point also contain a further, implicit demand that natural philosophers not merely repeat and rely on the *experientiae* furnished by Aristotle and by tradition, but rather make their own observations and conduct their own experiments, since by applying the inductive method to these data they will gain knowledge that is adequately confirmed and scientifically "evident."

In enunciating this methodological principle, Buridan almost anticipated the outlook of modern science. Once again, however, the discovery was essentially limited to the method itself, and no real use was made of it, apart from one or two exceptional cases. Time after time fourteenth-century philosophers were content to understand the manner of knowing without pursuing the knowledge itself.

This attitude produced—or perhaps derived from—an unusual deficiency in the "new physics" of the fourteenth century: no one ever measured anything. The philosophers not only refused, even in the simplest cases, to search for ways and means to make indirect measurements, they also ignored the chance to make direct measurements when this was clearly feasible. They were satisfied with approximate quantitative values in their experiments and induc-

---

23. The passage continues: "And he who does not wish to allow such statements in natural and moral science is not worthy to have a large part in them." This remark was clearly directed against Autrecourt.

tions, and in their *calculationes* they either used arbitrary magnitudes determined a priori or stayed on the abstract level of computations using letters alone. Given this attitude, the question is whether it arose from unwillingness or inability. Did the complete lack of measurement result from a renunciation of a really exact natural science and a willingness to be satisfied with a purely philosophical examination of method? Or was it, conversely, the inability to make exact quantitative measurements that produced the attitude?

I believe that the first interpretation is the correct one. Scholastic philosophers not only did not make any measurements in practice and did not develop any theory of measurement, they also maintained that really exact measurements are impossible in principle.[24] The reason for this attitude was, in the last analysis, a matter of world view. As mentioned earlier, these thinkers were convinced that everything in the world, including every abstract "intensive magnitude," has a completely determined measure that can be expressed quantitatively: "You have ordered all things in measure, number, and weight." Yet this same principle, which justifies every calculation no matter how far flung, also forbids measurement. The whole world may be numbered and measured in every detail, but only God possesses this knowledge. Humans cannot know and confirm the exact measure of things. This attitude applies not only to magnitudes of intensity, which are not, in fact, measurable in the way scholastic philosophers thought them to be, but also to the simplest form of measurement—the determination of length. Even here, scholastic philosophers were faced with a real difficulty, for there is no natural unit of measurement for describing and comparing spatial magnitudes. The fact that people were already completely familiar with conventional standards of measurement in practical life and had become used to the greater or lesser degree of exactitude that could be attained was of course irrelevant to the philosophers' theoretical deliberations. It is wholly characteristic of the mental outlook of late scholasticism that its representatives

24. For this see *Metaphysische Hintergründe*, p. 397 ff., and *Zwischen Philosophie und Mechanik*, p. 24 ff.

refused on theoretical grounds to accept arbitrary standards and approximate measurements as the basis of their epistemology. On the other hand, they would have nothing to do with any methodology that could only be based on such principles.

Thus they never took the final step that would have led from a purely philosophical view of nature to exact science. Nevertheless, it is no exaggeration to say that within the limits they set for themselves, that is, in their examination of the principles and methods that lead to an understanding of nature, fourteenth-century philosophers achieved some remarkable results. And it seems to me that these results are much more important than the rare and more or less disputable cases in which they anticipated some concrete physical theory.

Index

The Middle Ages

Edward Peters, General Editor

History of the Lombards. Paul the Deacon. Translated by William Dudley Foulke

Monks, Bishops, and Pagans: Christian Culture in Gaul and Italy, 500–700. Edited, with an Introduction, by Edward Peters

The World of Piers Plowman. Edited and translated by Jeanne Krochalis and Edward Peters

Felony and Misdemeanor: A Study in the History of Criminal Law. Julius Goebel, Jr.

Women in Medieval Society. Edited by Susan Mosher Stuard

The Expansion of Europe: The First Phase. Edited by James Muldoon

Laws of the Alamans and Bavarians. Translated, with an Introduction, by Theodore John Rivers

Law, Church, and Society: Essays in Honor of Stephan Kuttner. Edited by Robert Somerville and Kenneth Pennington

The Fourth Crusade: The Conquest of Constantinople, 1201–1204. Donald E. Queller

The Magician, the Witch, and the Law. Edward Peters

Daily Life in the World of Charlemagne. Pierre Riché. Translated, with an Introduction, by Jo Ann McNamara

Repression of Heresy in Medieval Germany. Richard Kieckhefer

The Royal Forests of Medieval England. Charles R. Young

Popes, Lawyers, and Infidels: The Church and the Non-Christian World, 1250–1550. James Muldoon

Heresy and Authority in Medieval Europe. Edited, with an Introduction, by Edward Peters

Women in Frankish Society: Marriage and the Cloister, 500 to 900. Suzanne Fonay Wemple

The English Parliament. Edited by R. G. Davies and J. H. Denton

Rhinoceros Bound: Cluny in the Tenth Century. Barbara H. Rosenwein

On the Threshold of Exact Science: Selected Writings of Anneliese Maier on Late Medieval Natural Philosophy. Edited and translated by Steven D. Sargent